UMBRIA
and the
MARCHE

a countryside guide
Third edition

Georg Henke

SUNFLOWER BOOKS

Third edition
Copyright © 2017
Sunflower Books™
PO Box 36160
London SW7 3WS, UK
www.sunflowerbooks.co.uk

ISBN 978-1-85691-501-4

Near Trevi (Walk 7)

Important note to the reader

In October 2016 a severe earthquake struck the border area of Umbria, the Marche and Latium, causing catastrophic damage to many places in this guide — like Norcia, Castellucio, Visso, Arquata del Tronto, and Amatrice. At time of last research (December 2016) all accommodation in the area was closed. It is not advisable to do Walks 14 or 27 to 32 before 2018.

Otherwise, we have tried to ensure that the descriptions and maps in this book are error-free at press date. The book will be updated, where necessary, whenever future printings permit. It will be very helpful for us to receive your comments (sent in care of the publishers, please) for the updating of future printings.

We also rely on those who use this book — especially walkers — to take along a good supply of common sense when they explore. Conditions can change fairly rapidly in the Umbria and the Marche, and *storm damage or bulldozing may make a route unsafe at any time*. If the route is not as we outline it here, and your way ahead is not secure, return to the point of departure. *Never attempt to complete a tour or walk under hazardous conditions!* Please read carefully the notes on pages 45 to 48, as well as the introductory comments at the beginning of each tour and walk (regarding road conditions, equipment, grade, distances and time, etc). Explore *safely*, while at the same time respecting the beauty of the countryside.

Cover photograph: Castelluccio
Title page: Porano, near Orvieto (Car tour 2)

Photographs: all photographs by the author
Maps: Sunflower Books
A CIP catalogue record for this book is available from the British Library.
Printed and bound England by Short Run Press, Exeter

Contents

4 Landscapes of Umbria and the Marche

The Castelluccio Plateau (Car tours 5 and 8, Walks 27-29)

Preface

'Italy's Green Heart' is the motto with which the small region of **Umbria** entices visitors. And it's true that the colour green dominates the landscape here more than in any other part of the Apennine peninsula — from the glistening silver-green olive groves above Lake Trasimeno to the dark green holm oak woods edging the Valle Umbra and Valnerina and up to the beech forests, mountain pastures and high grassy plateaus of the Monti Sibillini. This picture is not only true for Umbria, but also for the lesser-known neighbouring region of the **Marche** (apart from the built-up area on the Adriatic coast and immediate hinterland).

The most scenic corners of Umbria and the Marche often remain hidden from view if you're driving. The 37 walks described in this book lead deep into the untouched and sometimes surprisingly rugged landscapes in the geographical centre of Italy.

Softly undulating **Mediterranean low mountain ranges** extend to the west and east of the Apennine ridge, which stretches the length of Italy from north to south. Olive groves, vineyards, fields of sunflowers and corn, pastures full of sheep, oak forests and gorse macchia are strung together in a colourful procession. This landscape is embroidered with proud old farmsteads and a tapestry of small towns and villages with bold defence walls, old towers and gates clinging to the hillsides. The townscape of the Middle Ages has remained unchanged in many areas, as can be seen in places like Perugia, Assisi, Orvieto, Todi, Gubbio, Urbino or Ascoli Piceno. Together with the harmonious Mediterranean

Sant'Arcangelo, near Trevi (Walk 7)

countryside of the surrounding area, these settlements have attracted many visitors to central Italy in recent years.

On the other hand, the **high Apennine mountains of Umbria and the Marche** have remained largely unknown. On the whole, this region is far removed from the cheerful and gentle Italy with its olive groves and cypress-studded hills. Instead it's a lonely region, which sometimes appears more reminiscent of northern climes. There are thick deciduous forests and extensive high-mountain pastures; inhabitants of the remote small towns and villages meet visitors with reserved hospitality. Although there are steep ravines and huge mountains, the attraction of this region lies not only in the dramatic scenery, but even more so in its seclusion and silence. You climb up through shady mixed beech woods to mountain grasslands above the tree-line, where semi-wild horses sometimes roam beneath an endless blue sky. Narrow footpaths, seldom used, stretch across large flower-filled meadows and sparse mountain pastures; sometimes you will not meet another soul for hours, except for the occasional shepherd with his flock of sheep. The land appears light and far-reaching, the horizons endless — not unlike the background scenery of the well-known Italian Renaissance painters.

The main focal points of this guide are the two most beautiful areas of the Apennines in Umbria and the Marche — the idyllic, deeply-etched valley of **Valnerina** in Umbria and the legendary **Monti Sibillini** which rise to almost 2500m and lie mainly in the Marche. Although walks through the historically-important countryside of hills and low mountains are included, they only take up a relatively small section, because the book focuses on nature, not art and architecture. For example, the Adriatic coast in the Marche is so heavily built up that only **Monte Conero** near Ancona, with its coastal bays lined by limestone rock, is a worthwhile destination in this context.

Getting there and getting about

Direct **flights** from the UK go to Perugia, Ancona and Rimini (Ryanair). Ancona is the best Airport for the Marche and a two-hour drive from central Umbria. Rimini, near the northern

border of the Marche, is convenient for Urbino and Gubbio. Both
Rome airports offer a wide choice of international flights, with
central Umbria and the southern Marche a two-hour drive away.
Car hire is available at all airports and also at some railway stations
(but note that those offices are closed around noon, on Saturday
afternoons and Sundays). **Trains** run from Rome to Florence via
Orvieto and Terontola (change for Lake Trasimeno) and from
Rome to Ancona via Terni, Spoleto, Foligno, Fossato di Vico
(change for Gubbio) and Fabriano. From Foligno there are
connections to Florence via Assisi, Perugia and Lake Trasimeno.
A local line connects Perugia with Todi and Terni. On the east
coast, main line trains run from Bologna to Pescara, stopping at
Rimini, Pesaro (change for Urbino), Ancona, San Benedetto del
Tronto (change for Ascoli Piceno). Taking **your own car** (a
three-day drive from the UK) is only an option for a long visit.
Details of **local buses** are given are given with the walks.

Recommended reading
Landscapes of Umbria and the Marche is a countryside guide,
intended to be used in conjunction with a standard guide such as
Cadogan's *Tuscany, Umbria and the Marches; Rough Guide to
Tuscany and Umbria, Eyewitness Guide to Umbria* (good maps and
plans) or *Blue Guide Umbria* (the best cultural guide).

A country code for motorists and walkers
Please heed the following advice, whether you are out
motoring or walking.

• Because of the danger of forest fires, open fires should only
  be lit at specially provided barbecue areas; in dry weather,
  it is best to light *no* fires at all. Do not obstruct tracks which
  might be needed by fire-fighters.
• If at all possible avoid straying from the paths. Taking short-
  cuts across fields will damage the vegetation and will lead
  to the erosion of the main path. Do not walk across
  ploughed fields either.
• Do not pick wild flowers or cultivated plants and do not
  help yourself from fruit gardens or vineyards along the way.
  Small losses add up and will annoy farmers — who may close
  footpaths as a result.
• Ensure that gates are always closed, even if there are no
  animals in sight.
• Although some Italians still do not do this: take all rubbish
  away with you.
• Do not frighten animals or provoke watchdogs.
• Your behaviour towards local people should of course be
  considerate and polite. Respect private property and walk
  quickly past inhabited houses and farms.

Touring

The eight suggested tours open up the **most scenic areas** of Umbria and the Marche — from Orvieto and Lago Trasimeno in the west, to the mountains of Ascoli Piceno in the east. Well-known tourist locations have been chosen as starting points and, although natural beauty was the main consideration in choosing the tours, **many places of interest, small and large**, have been included — picturesque old towns and villages, fortified castles, Romanesque country churches, and isolated medieval monasteries. Italy would not be Italy if it were not possible to find interesting evidence of the country's artistic and cultural heritage in even the most remote small town. At the same time the tours will lead you to the **starting points of the walks** described in the second part of the book, so that you have many opportunities to don walking boots and get out into the great outdoors.

The descriptions of the routes have been kept brief and only contain minimal information about landmarks and places of architectural interest; detailed descriptions of these can be found in general travel guides. The **main emphasis is on leisurely car journeys** along scenic, quiet back roads and especially on the selection of **rewarding walks**.

On summer weekends people from the towns, laden with folding tables and chairs, escape from the sweltering heat into the mountains where they spend a lot of time together with their family, neighbours and friends at the *merenda*, the extensive outdoor meal with ham, salami, cheese, fruit and wine. Why not emulate the locals? Suggestions for some pleasant picnic areas are given at the beginning of each car tour. The location is shown on the touring map by the symbol *P*, printed in green. More and more **picnic areas** with wooden tables are being set up; these are shown in the text by the symbol ⧝.

Looking over the distances at the head of the tours, you can see that some of them could be completed in a single day, but take your time to enjoy fully the natural and man-made beauty. Bear in mind that roads in the hilly to mountainous central area of Italy are often winding and narrow, so that it is usually impossible to average more than 40km/h.

The large **touring maps** inside the back cover give an overview of the car tours, picnic areas and walks. It includes all the roads followed in the tours and is sufficient for route-planning. If you wish to purchase a further road map, I recommend the 1:200,000 Mair regional map ('Die General Karte', Sheet 8

Umbria/Marche), available from all good map stockists. It shows some minor unsurfaced roads and also highlights places of interest and outstanding natural beauty. Another excellent map (also at a scale of 1:200,000) is 'Umbria e Marche' published by the Touring Club Italiano; again, this is widely available in the UK and in Italy.

The **driving style** of the Italians sometimes appears a little chaotic. Traffic regulations are only rigidly adhered to if a traffic officer is nearby. So I would certainly advise you not to insist on your right of way! Always expect regulations like one-way traffic only, no overtaking or no turning to be openly flouted by other road users — despite the strict traffic police and high fines. Because of the many **police checks**, you should have all documents such as passport, driver's licence, car papers, insurance details etc, readily to hand.

Signposting is reliable on the whole, but sometimes can be confusing (when place names on the signposts of a defined route alternate at random between distant large cities and nearby small towns). **Green signs** lead to motorways. There are official **road numbers** which start with SS *(strada statale)* or SP *(strada provinciale)*, but on the ground you will only see these occasionally.

Parking places are limited within the tightly-built historic centres. In the larger cities in particular, it is best to follow the signs to the official car parks. *Black- and yellow-painted kerbstones* and lines indicate a no parking zone, *blue paint:* parking only against payment (parking meter), *white paint:* free parking. The following **speed limits** apply: in towns 50km/h, on country roads 90km/h, on trunk roads 110km/h and on motorways which have green signposts 130km/h. The **alcohol limit** is 0.5mg/l, significantly lower than in the UK. The wearing of **seatbelts** is law. **Lights** must be switched on, even during the day. The Italian Motoring Organisation (ACI) provides a **breakdown service** which is chargeable (emergency number 116, mobile 8 00 11 68 00).

The network of **petrol stations** is sparse in the countryside, so I recommend filling up before setting off. Most petrol stations will be closed on Sundays. The many **bars** in Italy are an important institution: not only is it possible to get espressos, cappuccinos and light snacks here, but there are also semi-public toilets, and it's possible to get information about absolutely everything!

A **key to the symbols** used in the touring notes is on the fold-out touring map at the back of the book.

Car Tour 1: MARE DEL UMBRIA — PERUGIA AND LAKE TRASIMENO

Perugia • Castel Rigone • Passignano sul Trasimeno • Castiglione del Lago • Chiusi • Citta della Pieve • Panicale • San Feliciano • Magione • Corciano • Perugia

168 km; about 5 hours' driving; allow an extra hour for the ferry crossing to Isola Maggiore and 30 minutes for the ferry crossing to Isola Polvese.
Walks en route: 1, 2
Picnic suggestions: The two tiny car-free islands on the lake are ideal for picnics. There are picnic tables and benches on **Isola Maggiore** (near Passignano, 30km) set among the olive groves above San Salvatore, and also by the path along the eastern shore. Another good spot is by the round tower at the southern tip of the lake, below the ruin of Villa Guglielmi. • On **Isola Polvese** (near San Feliciano, 135km), if you walk from the landing place towards the main building, then turn right in front of it, you will come to beautiful meadows with shady trees on the northern shore. There is also a small bathing beach, benches and tables on the path to the beach.

This tour leads from Perugia, Umbria's old capital with its many historic buildings, to Lago Trasimeno, the largest inland lake on the Apennine peninsula. The usually calm and vast expanse (128 sq km) of this 'Umbrian Sea' lies embedded in a landscape of soft green hills, where mainly olives and vines are grown. The 60km-long shoreline consists of a belt of reeds, field boundaries and small sandy beaches which are busy with bathers and campers in the summer. Various types of fish can be found in the lake, including pike *(luccio)*, perch *(persico)* and eel *(anguilla)*; this is how the San Feliciano fishermen make their living. While some unattractive new buildings mar the characteristic landscape, on the whole the Mediterranean idyll remains intact.

The tour runs through the harmonious highland all around Lake Trasimeno, at times skirting the shore, and takes in some old villages which lie further away but are worth a visit (Citta della Pieve, Panicale, Corciano). Be sure to include a boat ride to at least one of the two tiny islands in the lake: outside the summer tourist season and weekends, these are green oases of calm dotting the blue waters of Lake Trasimeno.

Leave the centre of **Perugia** *from the northern gate, Porta S. Angelo. Via Monteripido takes you to the suburb of* **San Marco**. *Continue straight through it, to the trunk road to* **Cenerente/Umbertide**.
The road to Umbertide leads down into a green wooded valley above which **Monte Tezio** rises in the north. Perugia's nearly 1000m-high local mountain is covered in vast meadows near the peak, which reveal a magnificent panorama. In **Cenerente** (5km) a minor road branches off towards Migiana di Monte Tezio, where Walk 2 to the Tezio peak starts.
After Cenerente first drive left along the valley, past the hill village of Capocavallo, then go right under a trunk road, following signs for **Preggio/Castel Rigone**.
You drive through sparsely inhabited farmland with olive groves, small meadows and forests. As you gain height, you have beautiful views across the undulating hills which stretch across to Lago

Passignano sul Trasimeno

Trasimeno. Once on the ridge, turn left to **Castel Rigone** (21km ✝♙). The church, Madonna del Miracoli, has a beautiful Renaissance door. Castel Rigone is a minute medieval village, which now houses a grand country-house hotel within its walls. The road then descends through olive groves and pastures full of gorse, with views to the vast, sparkling surface of Lake Trasimeno (☎), where the three little islands form dark green dots.

Passignano sul Trasimeno (30km *i*☐) is a holiday resort on the shore of the lake. This small town was the target for Allied air raids during the Second World War because of its aeroplane factory. Fortunately part of the compact medieval town centre, on a hill above the lake, remained intact. The piazza below the medieval castle ruin offers a wonderful view of the lake (☎). All year round ferries travel from here to **Isola Maggiore**★ (✝☐♙✕), an idyllic small island with a tiny village, an enchanting ruined villa (for which development plans are on the drawing board), a single road which never sees a car, and footpaths through rolling olive groves to lovely picnic places (see Walk 1).

From Passignano take the old country road which runs parallel to the expressway, heading towards Tuoro sul Trasimeno.

The hill village of **Tuoro sul Trasimeno** lies a short distance inland and is of little interest, except for the fact that in 217BC the well-known battle took place near this village in which the Romans suffered a major defeat at the hands of Hannibal. A signposted circular walk leads to the old battle sites. In summer busy bathing beaches and camping places stretch along the lake shore at the **Punta Navaccia** (38km ⚓) below Tuoro. Some 27 peculiar modern sculptures stand on the Campo del Sole nearby. There are also ferries

from here to Isola Maggiore.

*The country road continues past Tuoro, again a little above the shore and with views over the lake. At a fork, take the left turn to the unimpressive village of **Borghetto**, then follow the wide SS71 towards **Castiglione del Lago**. This road runs parallel with the western shore. Park outside the walls of Castiglione del Lago.*

The *centro storico* of **Castiglione del Lago**★ (54km *i*⚓●), with almost 15,000 inhabitants, is the largest settlement on the lake. It stands on a limestone ridge which extends some distance into the lake. Until the Middle Ages this was the fourth island in Lago Trasimeno, but the slowly-sinking water level eventually left Castiglione's rock connected with the shore. The town centre, with its well-preserved defence wall, old gates and square towers, still has a very medieval appearance. Worth visiting are the Palazzo della Corgna, a grandiose 16th-century Renaissance palace with beautiful frescoes, and the Rocca del Leone, an invincible fortress dating back to the 13th century, from where beautiful views across the lake and its islands can be enjoyed.

*At Castiglione's cemetery turn right off the SS71 on the minor road towards **Villastrada** via **Gioiella**; 1km before Villastrada turn right towards **Chiusi**. (3km before Chiusi you could take a detour to **Lago di Chiusi** by turning right after the railway line and then*

11

right again 4km further on.)
Past Castiglione the tour leaves the shore of Lago Trasimeno, which is not very attractive at this point, and detours west through Tuscany. You drive through calm, undulating countryside of cornfields pierced by the occasional pine or cypress. **Lago di Chiusi** (76km ✖) appears to the west of the ridge, a small protected reed-filled lake with some restaurants, where you can try freshly-caught fish. **Chiusi** (84km ●ⅡⅯ), with barely 10,000 inhabitants, traces its history back to Etruscan times, and many Etruscan necropoli have been unearthed in the vicinity. The archaeological museum near the cathedral gives a good insight into the history of these mysterious people, who reigned over middle Italy from the 7th to the 3rd century BC.
*Following signposts to **Perugia**, the tour continues on the main SS326, passing to the west of Chiusi to **Chiusi Scalo**, the modern district near the station. After crossing the railway line turn right on the SS71 in the direction of **Citta della Pieve**.*
Leaving the built-up plain behind, you quickly find yourself back in hilly Mediterranean countryside with vineyards, olive groves and pine forests. **Citta della Pieve**★ (95km *i*●ⅰ̇M) is a pleasant small country town. Its old centre was built almost entirely of brick and so presents a uniform picture in shades of red and brown. Medieval towers, gates and walls delineate the town's silhouette. While strolling through the narrow lanes you will come upon old palazzos and churches, as well as what is believed to be Italy's narrowest lane, the Vicolo Baciadonne. The famous Renaissance painter Perugino came from here, and one of his best-known works ('The Adoration of the Kings') hangs in a small church, the Oratorio Santa Maria dei Bianchi.
From Citta della Pieve drive 2km back

*on the SS71, then head right on a minor road through the hills, down towards **Moiano**. From here follow the main road east for 1km, then turn right uphill to **Paciano**. When you reach the outskirts, ignore the signs to Panicale and continue straight up a steep side-road, to the right of the old town wall.*
Paciano★ (●), another medieval village with towers and gates, is well worth a short walk. A protective wall encircles the compact old centre.
Back in the car, take a narrow road at the top end of the village, into olive groves.
This lovely route along the gently descending Monte Petravella offers distant views of Lago Trasimeno. You reach the picturesque village of **Panicale**★ (114km ●🖼) sheltering behind round brick walls. Walk up through the tightly-built old town to the 14th-century Palazzo del Podesta (town hall). From the front of its walls there are more fine views across Lago Trasimeno up to the old Tuscan hill town of Cortona.
*Leaving Panicale, follow signs towards **Perugia**. On the southeastern side of Panicale, turn left on the **Tavernelle/Castiglione** trunk road. Follow this uphill for 1km, then turn sharp right and take the narrow road towards **le Casalini**.*
The little-used road leads through the old hamlet of **Lemura** and down into a wide flood plain with fields and pastures, then continues through the new village of **Casalini**. East of the village, past the hill with a castle (Castello di Montalera; privately owned), you meet the main road along Lago Trasimeno. Follow this round the southeasterly tip of the lake. Beyond **Sant' Arcangelo,** with its large camping places, thick reed borders fringe the shore.
*North of **Monte Buona** turn left on the minor road which skirts the lake, heading towards **Monte San***

Corciano

Savino/San Feliciano/Monte del Lago.
Gently sloping olive groves grace the eastern shores of Lake Trasimeno, where you come upon three unassuming villages. A short trip into the seemingly deserted little **Monte San Savino** (🖼) is especially worthwhile at sundown, when the evening light is mirrored in the reed-covered lake. The more lively **San Feliciano** (135km **M**), close to the lake, is known as the fishermen's village: fishing has been the basis of their existence here for hundreds of years — a tradition vividly documented in the Museo della Pesca. I highly recommend the crossing from San Feliciano to the idyllic **Isola Polvese★** (🖼▉🛏). No cars are allowed on this nature reserve, with its ruined castle and monastery. It's an ideal place for picnics and quiet walks through beautiful countryside. There is even a small bathing beach.

North of San Feliciano the road passes the ruins of the **Castello di Zocco** (🖼), which was the most powerful fortress on Lago Trasimeno in the Middle Ages. The next village, **Monte del Lago★**, presents a lovely picture. Its low old stone houses stand huddled together on a mound above the water.

Leave the shore road at Monte del Lago and, level with the village, take the road heading up to **Magione**.
Follow this road up through olive groves to **Montecolognola** (🖼), a medieval village set on a hill. From here you can look across the vast waters of Lake Trasimeno for the last time. After the next small town, **Magione** (144km ▉), you come to a large castle which was built by the Knights of Malta in around 1420. Unfortunately, it's nearly always closed.

Beyond Magione follow the main road towards **Perugia**, *parallel with the expressway. New supermarkets and*

small factories in the valley provide a fleeting contact with the modern world. Approximately 7km past Magione follow the sign to the left, towards **Corciano**.
Leaving the built-up valley behind, you find yourself back in rural hilly countryside. The small, enclosed medieval village of **Corciano★** (154km ●♦M) appears almost deserted. But in spring, during the Primavera Corcianese (the festival of jugglers and musicians), these village lanes are full of life. The parish church of Santa Maria Assunta, the small church of San Cristofero (with adjacent farm museum), and the town hall (Palazzo Comunale) are worth a visit.

Drive east for 2km on the main approach road, then turn left on the road to **Umbertide**.
The tour continues through wooded highlands past the well-fortified Renaissance fortress of **Castello di Pieve del Vescovo** (▉) and down into the valley at the foot of Monte Tezio. Before reaching the new through road to Umbertide, turn right, back on the road you took at the start of the tour; this leads past the hill village of **Capocavallo**, back to **Perugia** (168km).

Car Tour 2: FROM ORVIETO TO TODI, VIA AMELIA

Orvieto • Civita di Bagnoregio • Civitella del Lago • Guardea • Lugnano in Teverina • Amelia • Santa Restituta • Todi • Titignano • Orvieto

192km; about 5-6 hours' driving. The roads are often narrow and winding; driving will be slow. To explore Todi thoroughly, you should allow two days for this tour.

Walks en route: 3, 4

Picnic suggestions: There are lovely meadows with far-reaching views across the valley of the Tiber around the **Castello del Poggio** by Guardea (67km). • The hill at **Amelia** (91km) is another good spot: from the highest point, near the quiet cathedral square, you have the best panoramic views across the hills of the Amerino (benches). Another excellent place for a break is the **Valley of the Rio Grande**, a stream below Amelia. A walk along its bank begins by the car park on the road to Cappuccini/Sambucetole (on the right, behind the bridge which crosses the stream). This path curves east and ends after about 10 minutes at an old dam with a small waterfall (benches and tables along the way). • Finally, from the edge of the small cobbled piazza in the tiny village of **Borgo di Titignano** (163km) there are views down to the sparkling surface of Lake Corbara, while at the entrance to the village a small cypress forest offers shade for outdoor picnics.

T his tour begins in Orvieto, spectacularly positioned on a volcanic rock and with a splendid gothic cathedral. We drive via the old hill town of Amelia and then continue through the sparsely populated uplands of southern Umbria, through which the Tiber flows. One of the highlights of the tour is the medieval town of Todi — described by one American city-planner as the very best example of urban planning, with ideal living conditions. The countryside en route, although lacking in drama, is most attractive on the whole. Cornfields, meadows, olive groves, vineyards and dark green macchia forests alternate in colourful succession, punctuated with intertwined old towns and villages built of natural stone.

*From **Orvieto Scalo**, the modern town near the station, take the road to **Bolsena** which runs along the south side of the volcanic rock. After 1.5km turn left across a ditch and then immediately right on the minor road towards **Porano**.*
The narrow road leads uphill through olive trees and past the twelve-cornered tower of the **Abbey of San Severo** (✝), eventually affording an open view to the Orvieto setting (📷). The hills are thickly covered with vines near the village of **Porano** (7km). The Orvieto Classico wine, which is produced here, is one of the best-

Orvieto: the cathedral

loved of Italian white wines.
*Continue on the country road from
Porano to **Bagnoregio**, just past the
border with Latium (Lazio). At the
entrance to this village/town, turn left
towards **Civita/Belvedere** and drive
for 1km to a car park. Crossing the new
valley bridge will take you to the Civita
di Bagnoregio, which can only be
reached on foot.*

From the edge of **Bagnoregio**
(17km) you enjoy unexpected views
of the neighbouring, extremely
picturesque, medieval **Civita di
Bagnoregio★** (☞), situated on a
steep volcanic ridge. The few houses
of the village (which is in danger of
collapsing) stand at the very edge of
steep cliffs. If you walk east out of
the village on the 'main road' from
the church square, you will soon
look into the deeply furrowed,
bizarrely eroded landscape of the
Calanchi.

*Head back for 3km towards **Orvieto**,
then turn right and drive via
Lubriano (which offers another view of
the volcanic rock of Civita) down into
the Tiber Valley, to the main SS448
Orvieto/Todi road. But before
continuing left towards Todi on the far
side of the motorway, take a short 2km
detour to the right on the SS205 to
Baschi.*

Baschi★ (35km ●♣) is a compact
old hill village with twisted cobbled
lanes and the remarkable Chiesa San
Nicolo.

The SS448 towards Todi follows
the shore of the Tiber reservoir, the
Lago di Corbara★. Its calm blue
surface lies between green wooded
slopes. But unfortunately the water
is not very clean, and it is said that
there are treacherous currents: two
reasons why you cannot swim in
this lake. But you can enjoy some
lovely views from the lay-bys along
the shore road.

Drive uphill on a winding road to
Civitella del Lago (47km ●☞), set
on a plateau. Its old walls rise high
above the shore of the lake. From

the centre of the village you get a
good views across the Lago di
Corbara to the sparsely populated
hill country of southern Umbria.
*Follow the secondary road towards **Todi**
and about 5km after Civitella turn
right on the road to **Montecchio**.*

The little-used road at first ascends
the slopes of Monte Croce di Serra
through Mediterranean holm oak
forests. On reaching the summit it
turns west and passes a grassy rest
area on the right edged with cypress
trees (☞). The road then descends
towards the Tiber Valley, above
which the walls of the old hill town
of **Montecchio** (●) appear.

*Below Montecchio take the SS205
towards **Guardea**, **Lugnano in
Teverina** and **Amelia**.*

This 25km run to Amelia is a
panoramic route high above the
valley, along the western slopes of
Monte Croce di Serra. Beyond
Montecchio the long Lago di
Alviano comes into view, a bird
sanctuary where the Tiber has been
dammed (open to visitors only on
Sundays).

Turn left on the edge of **Guardea**
and follow the narrow road (brown
sign: 'Castello') uphill for 3km to
the **Castello del Poggio** (67km
◼☞). Although it is not possible to
visit the castle, the meadows and
holm oak groves all around make
lovely picnic places with views of the
Tiber Valley.

Beyond Guardea it is worth taking
two detours to the right. The first
leads down to **Alviano** (◼◼), with
its Renaissance fortress flanked by
round towers, the second to the
tightly-knit medieval hill village of
Lugnano in Teverina★ (●♣☞).
The approach road, with its lovely
views to Lake Alviano, leads to the
Piazza della Rocca. From here it is
only a short walk to the *centro storico*
with the Chiesa Santa Maria Assunta,
a very well preserved Romanesque
country church.

From here continue through dark

green macchia forests; 10km past
Lugnano, Amelia's distinctive
silhouette appears unexpectedly after
a left turn (☞). The tightly-woven
houses of the ancient city of
Amelia★ (91km *i*⦿♦☞) stretch up
the steep mountainside. Enormous,
roughly-built polygonal walls dating
back to early Umbrian times still
form the basis of the old city walls.
Walk through the Baroque gate, the
Porta Romana, to the *centro storico*,
which stretches uphill to the
cathedral. From the quiet cathedral
square near the octagonal
Romanesque campanile you can
enjoy a wonderful panorama across
the green rolling countryside of the
Amerino.

*From Amelia drive back for 2km on the
SS205, then turn right after the bridge
across the Rio Grande on the minor
road towards Macchia, but after
200m turn right again, recrossing the
Rio Grande, and head towards
Cappuccini/Sambucetole.*
The narrow road offers far-reaching
views of the hill ridge and passes a
modest monastery, the **Convento
Cappuccini** (♦). It then continues
as an unsurfaced road *(strada
bianca)* for a short distance, running
downhill through the Rio Grande
Valley to the Narni/Todi road.
*Turn left towards Todi. After 2km
turn left again and, past Castel
dell'Acquila, turn left again. Past
Melezzole, on reaching the road
coming from Civitella del Lago, follow
this to the right via Izzalini and Fiore
towards Todi.*
This route leads through agricultural
countryside at the foot of a dark
green, long mountain chain. Fields,
meadows and small forests alternate
in this region, which has little in-
dustry. Positioned on the slopes are
tightly-knit small villages like tiny
Santa Restituta (111km ✍), where
Walk 4 to the almost 1000m-high
Monte Croce di Serra starts. This
can be reached via a 3km-long access
road beyond Castel dell'Acquila.

Todi★ (140km *i*⦿♦♟M) can be
seen from afar: the large dome of
the Chiesa Santa Maria della
Consolazione, built from pale stone,
shines out brilliant white in front of
the medieval town's silhouette. Park
by the Renaissance church at the
foot of the hill (car park). From here
a footpath fringed with pines and
cypress trees leads uphill into the
compact *centro storico*. This is where
you'll find Todi's lively centre — the
cathedral square, bordered by three
old *palazzos*. Allow a minimum of
half a day to see the sights.
*Leave Todi the way you came in. Then
continue on the western edge of town,
following signposts straight on towards
Orvieto. The winding road leads
downhill into the Tiber Valley, and you
cross the river at the old village of
Pontecuti. Continue for 500m on the
main road, then turn off right on the
secondary road towards Prodo.*
This secondary road runs north of
the Lago di Corbara through a
harmonious landscape of sparsely
populated, undulating Mediterranean countryside. You will not
pass a large settlement for about
40km. The road twists and turns
uphill past low-built old farms. As
you look back across vineyards and
meadows, Todi's prominent hill
comes into view (☞).
On reaching the top, turn left on a
dusty dirt track for about 3km to
Titignano (163km ■☞), a large
medieval farm *(fattoria)* framed by
cypress trees. A small cobbled piazza
forms the centre of the group of
houses, and from its edge you have a
wonderful view across gentle hills
down to the sparkling blue waters of
Lake Corbara. The shore can only
be reached on foot from Titignano
(Walk 3).
Return to the secondary road and
follow this winding, little-used route
past the village of **Prodo** (■✍),
overlooked by a Renaissance castle,
then continue past many vantage
points back to **Orvieto** (192km).

Assisi • Nocera Umbra • Colfiorito • Pettino • Trevi • Montefalco •
Bevagna • Spello • Assisi

168km, about 5 hours' driving; mainly on winding secondary roads, but about 15km on a narrow dirt track.
Walks en route: 5, 6, 7
Picnic suggestions: In the first part of the tour, 4km past Bandita Cilleni, there's a pleasant picnic place with tables and benches on the ridge near the old **chapel at the pass** (21km), with meadows, shady trees and far reaching views. • Beyond **Colfiorito** (60km) the route leads through a small wetland. Meadows along the road to Forcatura offer places to stop, with views of the marshy reed beds. • Midway through the tour, in the lonely **high valley of Pettino** (87km), you can find picnic places on stony meadows alongside the road. • Further along, on the edge of Valle Umbra, the square in front of the small church of **Santa Maria** near **La Bianca** (98km) is also very pleasant, with stone benches set among pine and olive trees below an old villa.

This route opens up central Umbria — the Valle Umbra and nearby mountain regions. The busy Umbrian plain, the ancient cultivated land, is surrounded by a ring of small medieval towns which are worth a visit. Apart from the well-known centre of Assisi, the picturesque town of St Francis, other towns not to be missed include Trevi, Montefalco, Bevagna and Spello. With their old towers, gates, Romanesque churches and palaces, they embody the proud ideal of the *libero comune*, the self-ruled free town of the high Middle Ages.

On the edge of the plain the mountains quickly rise to about 1000m, and you soon find yourself in sparsely populated regions. The character of the area changes the more you climb. The mountainsides exposed to the sun, just at the southern edge of the Valle Umbra, are Mediterranean in appearance, with olive trees, pine trees, holm oaks, cypress trees and macchia forests. Above are mixed forests, more reminiscent of central Europe and, higher still, you find yourself in open highlands with meagre meadows and mountain pastures.

*Leave **Assisi** from the Piazza Matteotti at the upper end of the old town and drive through the arched gate of the town's fortifications towards **Gualdo Tadino**.*
The road heads immediately into lovely countryside and leads along the slopes above the valley of the **Tescio** stream, at first through dark green Mediterranean vegetation — holm oaks, pine and cypress trees. After 2km the terrain opens out; the road ascends and offers wonderful views into the sparsely populated highlands north of Monte Subasio. Sub-Mediterranean deciduous woods with sycamores, beech and especially summer-green oaks now cover the mountain slopes — typical woodlands of the north Umbrian mountains.
*Two kilometres beyond the **Valico di Montemezzo Pass** (820m ▣), by the km17 marker and opposite a group of houses with a bar, turn right on the dirt road towards **Nocera Umbra/ Agriturismo Casa del Vento**. This strada bianca carries on for 3km to the **S. Maria Lignano** junction near a shrine. Past here continue for a further 3km on the road, which has some pot-holes, and follow the right-hand bend to*

17

*the group of houses called **Bandita Cilleni** on top of the ridge.*

You could take the tarmac road on the left into the valley of Nocera Umbra from here; however, the scenery is much finer if you carry straight on along the dirt road through the group of houses. Bear left at the next fork in the woods. Immediately afterwards, as you look south, you can see Assisi's castle. You also have a good view from a lovely picnic place by a **chapel** at the next pass (🚻⛩🏞), 4km beyond Bandita Cilleni.

*The dirt road continues for a further 2km through woods, to a T-junction. Turn left here and continue alongside the hillside **ruins of Postignano** down into the Topino Valley. Drive past the village of **Villa di Postignano**, which is where the tarmac begins, then continue to **Nocera Scalo**. From here drive left across the Rome/Ancona intercity railway lines uphill to **Nocera Umbra**.*

The silhouette of the historic town of **Nocera Umbra**★ (37km ⊙🚻M) is still very beautiful when seen from the distance, but within the town itself the terrible devastation from the 1997 earthquake is still very visible. The façades of the houses in the old town are obscured by metal scaffolding, and a ghostly emptiness pervades the cathedral square. Life takes place outside the old town gate.

*At the northern edge of town turn right towards **Macerata** and, once in the valley, after 2km take the secondary road on the right towards **Annifo/ Colfiorito**.*

The winding route ascends the wooded slopes and passes the modest health resort of **Bagni di Nocera**, well known for its mineral

18

water. Beyond Colle Croce the countryside opens out, the woods recede, and the road runs high above a plain, where differently coloured squares of lentil, corn and potato fields form geometric patterns (📷). The symmetrical bare cone of Monte Pennino (1570m) rises in the east above the valley. Passing through **Annifo**, which is also scarred by earthquake damage, you come to the intensively farmed agricultural **plateau of Colfiorito**. The products grown here are almost exotic for Italians — runner beans, mange tout, lentils and, in particular, a special type of red potato. The sheeps' cheese from Colfiorito also enjoys a good reputation. Farmers sell their produce from small carts by the roadside. The Piano di Colfiorito was the epicentre of the earthquake in 1997 and the village of **Colfiorito** (57km 🏨🍴 🍺) was largely destroyed.

*Follow the main SS77 right towards **Foligno**; then, on the outskirts of Colfiorito, turn right (north) and drive via **Forcatura** back to the SS77.*

The road towards Forcatura runs along a marshy lowland, the **Palude de Colfiorito**★, which is overgrown with reeds. This strictly protected wetland is an important nesting site for numerous types of birds. In early summer flowering poppies paint the surrounding fields and meadows bright red.

*Stay on the trunk road until you reach the village of **Serrone**, then turn left towards **Casenove/Sellano**. (Or, to get to the start of Walk 6, carry straight on to Pale/Belfiore near Foligno.) After the km6 marker, bear right and drive via **Pettino** towards **Campello Alto** on the edge of the Valle Umbra.*

Beyond Serrone a quiet road takes you through a wooded valley with small villages and uphill into the desolate highlands at the foot of the Monte Serrone (1426m). The high narrow valley of Pettino is framed

Near Montefalco

by bare round mountaintops. Sheep and cows graze on the sparse pastures around the scattered houses of the village. Up here one feels a very long way away from the Mediterranean Umbria with its olive groves and vineyards.

Turn right in front of the small church at **Pettino** (87km) and drive past the group of houses in the west (✗ ☛). Looking northeast, you have a wonderful view across the valley from Pettino to the distant Monti Sibillini. You then follow a narrow winding road downhill through woods towards Valle Umbra. After a left-hand bend you catch a glimpse across dark green pines and holm oaks down onto the Umbrian plain (☞). Eventually the perfectly preserved wall encircling the fortified medieval village of **Campello Alto** (◼) emerges below the road.

As the road branches, bear left past the Campello Alto turn-off and continue further downhill, now through olive groves, towards the plain. In the village of La Bianca follow the sign in front of the church ('SS Flaminia'). This leads to the Via Flaminia trunk road, where you turn right and continue towards Foligno.

Some 2km outside La Bianca turn right on the small Via Santa Maria, for a short (1km) detour along a tree-lined lane to the **Chiesa Santa Maria**. While not noteworthy in itself, this small church is beautifully positioned near a manor house, among olive trees and pines (♱ ⋒).

You reach the Via Flaminia (SS3) near the **Fonti del Clitunno ★** (100km ☛). A clear spring emerges here from the forest floor and forms a calm pool. The Roman writer Pliny the Younger and, later, Lord Byron, described the special magic of this place. However, in those days you could not hear the traffic noise in the background!

A few kilometres further along, near the roadside village of **Pissignano** (☛), the small **Castello di Pissignano** (◼) rises on the right. Like Campello Alto, this is a well-preserved fortified medieval village. Immediately after Borgo Pissignano, follow signs left towards **Vecchio Mulino**, and by turning off the main road you reach this restored mill near the **Tempietto del Clitunno** (♱), an early Romanesque church in the form of an ancient temple.

Drive straight on, first parallel with the main road, then for a short distance on the main road. Then turn right on a minor road and drive uphill via Bovara towards Trevi. About 2km before Trevi turn left off the new bypass, then turn right and drive in a circle all the way round the village centre, to the car park at the entrance to the old centre.

A wonderful panorama presents itself on the approach to the small town of **Trevi ★** (109km *i* ● ♱ ◼ M; Walk 7). You get a view of the closely-knit, very picturesque old town which stretches all the way up the hill. In front of the walls silvery glistening olive groves cover the wide terraced slopes. While Trevi does not offer any remarkable places of interest, a walk through the *centro storico* with its old lanes is still worthwhile. Near the monastery of San Martino, on the edge of town, you will have wide-ranging views.

Leave Trevi on the same road that you came on. Below the town, take the road to the right, downhill. This leads past the large Renaissance church of Madonna delle Lacrime, with frescoes by Perugino, to the new roadside settlement of Borgo Trevi on the plain. Here turn left on the SS3 Via

19

Flaminia but, immediately, take the right fork signposted to **Montefalco**. *After crossing the railway and the expressway, when the road bends left, carry straight on uphill on a narrow road via* **Fabbri** *towards* **Montefalco**.

As you look back over the valley you can see the striking silhouette of Trevi again — but ahead of you your next destination already steals your attention: Montefalco, on a hill above the Valle Umbra. When you get to the village of **Fabbri** (∎), overlooked by a square castle tower, you will have left the heavy traffic of the plain behind. You now come into a friendly, undulating country-side, with small fields, olive groves and vine-clad hills. The narrow road up to Montefalco is mainly lined with vineyards. This is where the famous Rosso di Montefalco and Sagrantino wines are produced. **Montefalco★** (121km *i*●♣🏠M) describes itself as the 'Ringhiera dell'Umbria' — Umbria's balcony. A walk around the old town wall offers far-reaching views across the Valle Umbra, to the old hill towns of Assisi, Spello and Trevi. The central point of the old town is right at the top, the round Piazza del Comune, with a town hall dating back to 1270. Here you can taste the locally produced wines in two wine bars *(enoteca)*. The deconse-crated Chiesa di San Francesco, a few steps below, houses the extensive collection of the municipal art gallery.

From Montefalco follow signs to **Foligno** *and, after 2km, at* **Monte-pennino**, *turn left onto the smaller road to* **Bevagna**.

The small town of **Bevagna★** (128km *i*●♣), completely encircled by a wall, lies on the edge of the plain. This is another fascinating old town, with architectural treasures dating from antiquity to modern times. Here too, a walk around the tight kernel of the *centro storico* is highly recommended. The Piazza

Silvestri is one of the most authentic Middle Ages squares in Umbria. *Follow the main road towards* **Foligno**. *On the edge of town, at the traffic lights, turn left (at the km1 marker) on the Viale Firenze and leave Foligno off to your right. The road runs parallel to the railway line, then turns left across the railway and reaches* **Spello**. *Turn right here on the main road, then immediately turn left towards* **Collepino**. *This takes you to car parks below the town wall.*

Spello★ (144km *i*●♣🎭🏠M), at the foot of the Monte Subasio and the last of the medieval hill towns on this tour, makes a particularly lovely picture. Its beautiful silhouette rises above the plain like a mountain of stone. In the main church of Santa Maria Maggiore you can enjoy lively frescoes by the Renaissance painter Pinturicchio. The nearby Porta Venere dates back to Roman times (1st century). Winding, stepped lanes stretch above the town's decorative theatre, the Teatro Subasio. From the Belvedere viewpoint, high above, you have good views across the busy Valle Umbra to the mountains of middle Umbria.

Now follow narrow roads on the slopes of Monte Subasio, watching out for oncoming traffic, to make your way back to Assisi via **Collepino**, **San Giovanni** *and* **Armenzano**.

Drive through the olive groves of Spello uphill to **Collepino** (●∎🏠), a small old mountain village with more fine views to the Valle Umbra and the Apennine mountains by Nocera Umbra. Some maps still show a panoramic road from Collepino across Monte Subasio, but this is no longer motorable all the way. However the tarmac road which leads around the north side of the mountain gives ample far-reaching views to the mountains of northern Umbria en route back to **Assisi** (168km).

Car Tour 4: FROM SPOLETO THROUGH THE MONTI MARTANI INTO THE SOUTHERN VALNERINA

Spoleto • Carsulae • Cesi • Arrone • Labro • Lago di Piediluco • Cascata delle Marmore • Ferentillo • San Pietro in Valle • Scheggino • Spoleto

148km; about 4-5 hours' driving.
Important: *enquire in advance about the opening hours of the Cascata delle Marmore (mainly in the afternoons). At weekends these falls are very busy.*
Walks en route: 8-12, 13 (Variation)
Picnic suggestions: At the northern end of the extensive grounds surrounding the ruins of **Carsulae** (27km) there are lovely oak-shaded meadows. • 5km further on, at the entrance to **Cesi**, a sign indicates a secondary road off left to the small church of **Sant'Erasmo**, on a terraced meadow with views to Monte Terminillo (2200m). Some 250m higher up the road there are picnic areas with benches and tables.
• At the highest point of the centre in **Labro** (70km) you can sit in a small meadow near the medieval walls and look out towards the Monti Reatini.

The first ranges of the Apennines, with their green wooded slopes, rise near the old town of Spoleto. At the start of this tour we drive through their first westerly outposts, the Monti Martani. These 'Martian Mountains' were settled in antiquity: on the highest, Monte Torre Maggiore, there are the foundations of an early Umbrian holy place on the summit and, on the slope below, the ruins of Roman Carsulae are found near the ancient Via Flaminia. Other scenic highlights are the blue Lago di Piediluco and especially the Valnerina, the idyllic valley of the Nera. The glistening green river snakes its way downstream through steep mountains. The Cascata delle Marmore, in the lower valley, are considered the most beautiful waterfalls in Italy, while the beautifully-sited San Pietro in Valle, north of Ferentillo, is one of the best preserved Romanesque monasteries. There are also many medieval villages in this region; at least ten lie en route, including Cesi, Labro and Ferentillo.

*Near the station in **Spoleto** take the road towards **Todi/Acquasparta**. North of the railway underpass, turn left towards **San Nicolo**. Drive through the plain, unfortunately spoilt by development, until you reach the main road to **Acquasparta**, which you follow for 2km, past **Baiano**. Then turn left on the minor road to **Fogliano**. Shortly before Fogliano, do not follow the signpost to Giuncano; instead, before reaching the houses, turn left on the unsurfaced road to **Macerino**.*
Past **Baiano** we leave the busy and densely built-up Valle Umbra. The narrow road to Fogliano leads uphill

Portaria

through lovely countryside into the lonely highlands of the **Monti Martani**. Small forests, meadows and pastures present a colourfully woven tapestry of the countryside. There are a few villages, modest in appearance, along the route. One of them is the small village of **Macerino** (◉), at the end of a short access road; its old walls rise above a cypress-studded hill.

Returning from Macerino, turn right; then, as the road branches, fork right on the little-used unsurfaced road towards **Portaria**.

This easily-driven dirt road runs through shady deciduous woods for a while, then descends to the plain of Acquasparta, with good views (☏). On the way you pass the small village of **Portaria** (◉☎☏), one of many little-known but well-preserved medieval Umbrian villages.

Below Portaria turn left and drive to the ruins of **Carsulae**. *Continue via* **Cesi**, *from where you take a detour to* **Sant'Erasmo**, *and then drive on towards* **Terni**.

Poets of the antiquity praised the scenic location of **Carsulae★** (27km ☏☏). The few remaining ruins of this once-important Roman town today lie alone on a wide terraced meadow under the shade of large trees. The symmetrical, dark green ridge of the Monti Martani forms the background. Even if you are not interested in ruins, it's worth taking a walk around the field. Apart from the remains of a theatre, amphitheatre, town gate and two tombs, there is a well-preserved piece of the Via Flaminia, the ancient trunk road dating from 220 BC which connected Rome with the Adriatic port of Fano.

The buildings of medieval **Cesi** (32km ◉☏☎☏; Walk 9) huddle together high against the mountain slope. Walk though the steep lanes, to the parish church of Santa Maria (altar painting and wooden

sculpture), then climb higher, for a wonderful view from the terrace of the bar on the Piazza Umberto I. From the northern entrance to Cesi a yellow sign shows the way to the access road up to Sant'Erasmo. Even on the way up you have wonderful views over the countryside, but the views are even better from the meadow in front of the small medieval church of **Sant'Erasmo** (☏☏☏☏). The square in front of Sant'Erasmo was created from the large boulders of an ancient Umbrian holy place. Further up, on the top of the 1120m-high Monte Torre Maggiore, the foundations of another temple dating back to the ancient Umbrian population have been unearthed. (Walk 9 visits Carsulae, Monte Torre Maggiore and Sant'Erasmo.)

The road from Cesi towards Terni at first runs along the slopes of the Monti Martani, which drop steeply to the west. The limestone shines brightly through the dark green holm oak woods, and further down, olive groves cover the hills.

Less attractive is the landscape around **Terni**. *Pass to the left of this town, which was destroyed during the Second World War and which now spreads far into the surrounding countryside. On the edge of town, at the first round-about, first follow the signs towards* '**Rieti**' *and then* '**SS3 Spoleto**'. *Stay on the expressway for 5km, at which point it reverts to the old country road east of Terni. Some 6km further on, turn right on the secondary road towards* **Montefranco/Arrone**.

The narrow road snakes uphill to the crest of the pass, then leads down towards **Montefranco** (◉☏), another tightly-knit old village in lovely countryside. From here drive all the way into the valley of the river Nera, the **Valnerina**. In the valley you cross the road from Terni to Visso and then continue to the old hill town of **Arrone** (55km ◉☏). This is another good place to

from the Gola di Valnerina and then turn left on the narrow road towards **Saccovescio/Borgo Preci**.

From the Valnerina you now head into a side-valley, the **Valle Casto-riana**. Here too you come upon a varied landscape, with small villages standing between poplar meadows and pastures, against the backdrop of the bare, high Monti Sibillini (☐). The first settlement in the valley, the tightly-woven hill village of **Preci** (86km ⊙▲✕✈), rises above pastures. It won fame all over Europe back in the 16th century, because of its surgeons specialising in eye operations.

Drive through **Borgo Preci** *towards* **Norcia**.

Some 3km beyond Borgo Preci, in **Piedivalle**, a short detour left uphill leads to the beautifully sited 12-16C monastery of **Sant'Eutizio★** (89km ✝M), where Preci's surgeons were trained. Walk 14 begins here. Past Piedivalle the old village of **Campi Vecchio** (⊙), built against the mountain slope, comes into view. Below it the valley road continues past the old church of **San Salvatore** (✝; usually locked) to a bar. This is where the access road branches off uphill into the village. The main church of Sant'Andrea overlooks the Valle Castoriana from an airy viewing balcony.

The route in the Valle Castoriana reaches its highest point at the **Forca d'Ancarano**. From the pass the road descends with fine views into a wide valley basin. Totally encircled by a medieval wall, **Norcia★** (104km *i*⊙✝▲ M) has for centuries been one of the most remote towns in the Apennines. The centre is the lovely Piazza San Benedetto with the Palazzo Comunale (town hall), the basilica of the town's patron saint (San Benedetto, founder of the Benedictine Order), and the Castellina, the Renaissance castle of the pope's governors. Norcia is

known throughout all of Italy for its speciality foods: sausages, sheep's cheese, trout, mushrooms, lentils, and expensive truffles.

Before you return to Spoleto, a detour up to the magnificent Castelluccio Plateau is a must. To get there, leave Norcia by heading south towards **Ascoli Piceno/Cittareale**. *After 3km turn left and left again at the next two forks (both signposted to* **Castelluccio**). *(But to get to the Forca Canapine pass for the start of Walk 28, turn right at the second fork (125km).)*

The road steadily gains height as it heads uphill in wide curves. The woods gradually retreat, and across the now-barren slopes you can see all the way to the Norcia basin with its cornfields. From the pass beyond the Rifugio Perugia you have an amazing view: all of a sudden you are confronted with a large uninhabited plateau framed by barren mountains (☐).

The **Piano Grande di Castel-luccio★** is a dried-up lake dating back to the Ice Age, a vast empty landscape reminiscent of the South American highlands. Few trees stand among the fields and pastures. Right at the top of one of the mountains, at a height of 1450m, the few houses of the only village huddle together, seeking shelter in each other's company: this is remote **Castelluccio** (134km ▲✕✈; Walks 27, 29), which used to survive mainly from growing *lenticche*, a much valued, special type of lentil. Nowadays walkers, hang-gliders and cross-country skiers seek it out.

Retrace your route until you are 3km short of Norcia, then turn left towards **Savelli/Cittareale**.

Drive through a wide, high plateau and past villages with buildings still collapsed since the 1979 earthquake — buildings like the large Renais-sance church of **Madonna della Neve** (✝) by **Castel Santa Maria**, now reduced to mere rough walls.

Norcia

Enjoy another distant view of the barren Monti Sibillini from the pass of **Forca di Civita**; then, 1km further on, turn right on a minor road which descends between wooded slopes to the pilgrimage town of **Cascia★** (184km *i♥*). Everything here revolves around Santa Rita, the patron saint of maids and housewives. In 1940 a kitschy pilgrimage church was built in neo-Byzantine style.

Leave Cascia by heading southwest towards Rieti/Leonessa and follow the road uphill for 12km, then turn right towards Monteleone di Spoleto.
From the highest point in Cascia you can look back and catch a fine view of its group of old houses before driving across a small plateau to the pass of **Forca Rua la Cama**. From here the road descends through a narrow part of the valley and onto the plain, dominated by majestic Monte Terminillo (2216m), Lazio's highest mountain. Remote **Monteleone di Spoleto★** (198km ●■M🎦) is a friendly place set on a hill with lovely views. The old centre lies in the upper town, and steps lead up to the small piazza near the San Francesco monastery. The find of an Etruscan war chariot caused an archaeological sensation in the village; a copy of it is on show in the church of San Gilberto.

Take the secondary road towards Spoleto.
You soon have a superb view back to the hill of Monteleone (🎦).
At the next fork (206km) bear right towards Usigni/Cerreto di Spoleto. (A detour to the left here leads to tiny Gavelli, where Walk 13 starts.) Driving via wonderfully-sited Usigni and Poggiodomo, reach a further fork (212km) and bear left. This will take you via Mucciafora/Vallo di Nera towards the Valnerina. A short excursion to the right leads to the Madonna della Stella hermitage, a good picnic spot.
You pass the old villages of **Rocca-tambura** and **Mucciafora**; then the asphalt ends and you arrive on a lonely plateau with sparse pastures, from where you have a final view of the Monti Sibillini (🎦). The winding, little-used unsurfaced road then leads downhill through woods into medieval **Vallo di Nera★** (224km ●♥) — probably the Valnerina's most attractive village. The main, 13th-century church of Santa Maria, richly painted with frescoes, is worth a visit.
Below Vallo di Nera turn left on the Valnerina valley road, the SS209.
Drive past pretty **Castel San Felice** (●♥) with its Romanesque church on the river bank until just beyond **Sant'Anatolia di Narco** (✕■). Then take the new tunnel, quickly arriving back in **Spoleto** (242km).

Car tour 6: THROUGH THE CENTRAL APENNINES VIA LITTLE-KNOWN MOUNTAINS AND HISTORICAL TOWNS

Gubbio • Pietralunga • Piobbico • Cagli • Fonte Avellana • Sassoferrato • Frasassi Gorge • San Severino Marche • Fabriano • Monte Cucco • Gubbio

292km, 8-9 hours' driving, mainly on winding secondary roads. This is a two-day tour, with hotels in Cagli, San Vittore Terme, San Severino Marche, Matelica and near Monte Cucco.

Walks en route: 15, 18-25

Picnic suggestions: countless pleasant picnic places can be found in the secluded forest landscape of the Apennines. Shortly before reaching Piobbico (56km), for example, you could take a 10-minute walk to the **valley of the Rio Vitoschio**, where you can relax under the steep rock face of les Portes near Vitoschio stream. • Other good spots can be found all around the **monastery of Fonte Avellana** (94km) beyond Cagli, from where you have a wonderful view of the deserted mountain world. Picnic sites with tables and benches have been set up 2km below the abbey, near the Cesano stream. • Near the secluded little **monastery of Val di Castro** (158km), you can sit on the sloping meadows. • Beyond Monte San Vicino the route follows an unmade road for a short way. When the tarmac starts again (170km), two tracks on the right lead through beech forests to the **meadows of Canfaito**, where you can picnic in the shade of large leafy trees with view to the Monte San Vicino. • The sparse, stony slopes above tiny **Elcito** (173km) are also good for picnicking, with good views over the rooftops to the Abruzzi region (but no shade). • Two kilometres beyond Esanatoglia (216km) an access road to the left leads uphill to the church of **San Cataldo** which enjoys lovely views, and there is a small area with rocks to sit on higher up. • Good picnic spots abound near **Monte Cucco** (257km). You could, for example, walk north along the forest path between holiday homes above the Albergo Monte Cucco for 20 minutes, then walk round the side of the hill and down into the **Valle di San Pietro Orticheto**, where there are meadows and shady trees near the stream (see Walk 22).

The mountains of the central Apennines, with their deciduous forests, grazing pastures and remote small towns and farms are more reminiscent of a central than a southern European landscape. Indeed this region has mostly been left blank on Italy's tourist maps. But for the lover of unspoilt nature, there is much to discover — from vast treeless mountain meadows covered in wild flowers to deeply-etched, rocky valleys and shady forests with large beech trees and oaks. With the exception of Gubbio, the small towns of the region are little known, but — as everywhere in Italy — they hold many interesting works of art and architecture.

This tour explores the most scenic areas of the central Apennines from north to south: the secluded natural landscape of Monte Nerone near Piobbico, Monte Catria near Cagli (with the old abbey of Fonte Avellana), Monte Cucco with its wonderful beech forest set below a vertical rock face, and the limestone gorge of the Sentino with the spectacular grottos of Frasassi.

*Leave **Gubbio** by heading northwest towards **Umbertide/Citta di Castello**. Follow the SS219 past the km30 marker, then turn right on the secondary road towards **Pietralunga**.*

The route at first runs for several kilometres through the built-up plain of Gubbio with its cement works, then enters the green valley of the Torrente Assino, which we soon leave again by taking the secondary road to Pietralunga. The route continues for some kilometres along a ridge, with good views across the wooded **Apennines** to Monte Nerone (1525m) and Monte Catria (1701m). Ignoring a signpost to the left, continue on the ridge road for a further 3km, then head downhill along a winding road to **Pietralunga** (22km ⬛). This pleasant village still has some old walls and towers, but no other noteworthy sights.

*In the west, below the village, turn right on the country road north towards **Fano**.*

This little-used road rises steadily uphill through wide woodlands with pine, oak and beech trees. Take the signposts warning of deer crossing the road seriously; there are many deer in these forests. Beyond the crest of the pass the road descends into the green valley of the Torrente Certano, where you turn left to **Pianello** (38km ⬛). Continue along the western side of Monte Nerone, enjoying good views along the way. Make your way down into the valley of the Biscubio — via **Massa** (40km), where Walk 19 begins, and **Serravalle di Carda** (⬛✕⬛). Here the landscape changes a little. Grey- to red shimmering rock emerges everywhere, and the terrain now appears wilder and more barren (⬛).

*Joining the SS257 Citta di Castella/ Fano road in the Biscubio Valley, follow it east towards **Piobbico**.*

The road to Piobbico/Fano soon leads into a narrow valley where it skirts the Biscubio, a mountain torrent which winds its way downhill at the foot of sheer rocks. Steep Monte Nerone, which rises to almost 1500m, rises in the south — its summit unfortunately marred by a plethora of aerials. But once you reach the north side of the mountain, you will find that its lower slopes harbour small tributaries of the Biscubio, flowing with water. The countryside is unspoilt here, as you can see in the **valley of the Rio Vitoschio** 3km before Piobbico (58km; yellow signpost). This is the goal of Walk 18.

Piobbico (61km ⬛⬛) is a small, little-visited town at the confluence of the Biscubio and Candigliano. The oldest part of the town, the *castello,* stands alone above a bend in the Candigliano. The Rocca Brancaleoni, a well-preserved medieval castle, stands guard at the highest point.

*About 1km east of Piobbico turn off the SS257 which now heads towards Fano; turn right on the minor road towards **Cagli**.*

The narrow road leads through rugged terrain along the north side of Monte Nerone. All around you, arid, rocky soil can be seen through the green of the forest. Beyond **Acquanera** the church of San Lorenzo and a castle ruin, the **Rocca Leonella** (⬛⬛), can be seen on the mountain ridge to the left of the road. Below the ruin the Fosso dell'Eremo flows through a deeply etched valley.

Drive on through the almost-abandoned hamlets of **Bacciardi**, **Cardella** and **Fosto**, and then the village of **Secchiano** in the Bosso Valley, then follow the stream between wooded slopes until you arrive in **Cagli**★ (77km *i*⬛⬛). Like nearly all towns and villages in the Marche, this friendly little place, set on a hill above the Burano Valley, has a tightly-knit *centro storico* with a central piazza and

Walk 18: the path above the Rio Vitoschio and (right): stormy-day view from Frontone Castle, with rainbow

various *palazzos* and old churches. A short stroll will no doubt uncover something of interest.

*Below the village centre in Cagli, turn east off the Rome/Fano trunk road onto the road which heads across the Burano river towards **Pergola**; then, 2km out of Cagli, take the minor road to **Frontone**.*

The road winds through meadows along the northern slope of Monte Catria (1701m). The **Castello di Frontone** (▆☐), set on a hilltop, can be seen from afar. In the hamlet of **Buonconsiglio** follow the brown signpost 'Il Castello' to the left and drive all the way up to the castle along a narrow road. You have wonderful views from the village square below the castle — to the dark heights of Monte Catri, the almost equally high Monte Acuto in the south, and across the wide rolling countryside of the Marche.

*At the crossroads at the foot of the castle hill, drive right downhill into the village of **Frontone**, then turn left on the main road and immediately follow the signpost 'Foce' to the right, to continue towards **Fonte Avellana**.* This small road leads into a narrow river valley and then climbs in

curves up the mountainside. The horizon in the west is defined by the steep slopes of Monte Catria and Monte Acuto which rise from the valley. The road narrows again just after you rise over the pass of Forchetta, where Walk 20 begins. Shortly afterwards the monastery of **Fonte Avellana**★ (94km ☖▆☐) suddenly comes into view, its setting remote and pristine. This low-built medieval monastery, constructed from local stone, stands out against a background of deserted mountain ranges — a sight reminiscent of times long past. For over 1000 years monks of the Camaldule Order have lived here, far, far away from the hubbub of the towns. You can visit the monastery rooms on a guided tour.

Below Fonte Avellana the now-slightly wider road continues through the rocky, narrow valley of the Cesano. Small meadows alongside the roaring stream make ideal picnic spots (⌐).

Take the next right-hand fork towards Isola Fossara, from where you continue left on the valley road until you reach Sassoferrato.

The road ascends to a pass from where you have more wonderful views into the untouched country-side around Monte Catria, almost Alpine in appearance. Continue below the steep side of the moun-tain, past the simple Romanesque church of **Badia di Sitri** (☦), to **Isola Fossara** (104km) in the **Sentino Valley**. Then follow the course of the river east through high wooded mountains. Near the medieval abbey of **Sant'Emiliano** (☦), a road turns off right (109km) and runs via Perticano to San Felice,

Fonte Avellana Monastery (Walk 20)

where Walk 22 begins.

Continue through the ever-wider Sentino Valley until you reach **Sassoferrato★** (120km ●▢M). The interesting, old, upper town (Castello) can be seen from afar, rising on a mountain ridge. Nowadays everyday life takes place in the lower town (Borgo), although quiet Castello, with its old stone façades, was the town's centre in the Middle Ages, as evidenced by the two town halls on the vast main square.

From the bridge across the Sentino in Sassoferrato take the valley road north of the Sentino towards Ancona. After 4km bear right towards Grotte di Frasassi.

You continue to follow the course of the Sentino through the green valley. Ignore the left turn to Arcevia. Beyond this turn-off two access roads head north uphill: the first (127km) goes to Monticelli, where Walk 23 into the Valle Scappuccia begins, the second to Genga (●), a small medieval *borgo* set on a hill above the valley. Beyond the Genga turn-off the mountains above the Sentino move closer together. The road, which follows the course of the river, enters a short gorge, the **Gola di Frasassi**, with vertical limestone walls. At the entrance to the gorge, you pass a small lay-by on the left (near a well): from here you can take a walk of about 15 minutes to the pilgrimage church of **Beata Vergine** (or Madonna di Frasassi), built into a large cave. The main attraction of the Frasassi Gorge, however, is hidden deep in the rocks of the limestone mountain — the **Grotte di Frasassi★** (136km ∩☦ ⛰). This is a huge cave network with bizarre stalactites and stalag-mites — a fascinating phenomenon of nature.

In the spa town/village of San Vittorio Terme (137km), with its small fortified medieval church, turn left on *the minor road towards **Pierosaro/Cerqueto**. (The old country road along the Esino River and towards the coast via the gorge of Gola della Rossa is closed until further notice because of quarrying. But Walk 24 offers a good opportunity to explore the Gola della Rossa and the surrounding woodlands.) As you reach the first houses of **Cerqueto**, take the unsignposted and unsurfaced road heading north.*

This leads around the northern side of Monte Murano, then passes a picnic site with views into the valley at Avacelli (⌂) and meets up with a tarmac road which you follow downhill towards Serra San Quirico.

The older part of **Serra San Quirico★** (145km ◉🅟🗺), with its tightly-clustered old houses, rises on a hill above the Esino Valley. An idyllic small square with a fountain, near the town hall, forms the focal point, and from an archway you can enjoy fine views across the river valley into the harmonious highlands of the Marche.

*In the lower, new part of Serra San Quirico, turn right on the road to **Fabriano**. Drive past the railway station, then take the first fork to the left, towards **Poggio San Romualdo**; you cross the railway, the expressway and the river.*

The road climbs uphill in twists and turns. At several points you have a good view of the old part of Serra San Quirico (🗺). Following the signposts to Poggio San Romualdo, you arrive on a green upland with meadows and fields. Near San Giovanni the old hill village of Castello Precicchie (▮) appears in the east below the road; near **Vigne** symmetrical Monte San Vicino comes into view — at 1479m, it's the highest mountain in this area. About 2km before coming into Poggio San Romualdo, turn left on a narrow road which descends into a valley basin. The tarmac finishes near the isolated medieval

monastery of Val di Castro (162km ✝), surrounded by meadows.

Just about 50m before the monastery bear right on the unsurfaced road signposted 'San Vicino'.

This dirt track continues for a short distance into the valley (drive slowly: there is a danger that cows may run in front of the car!), then bends left high along the slope. From here you have a really good view down to Val di Castro (🗺). When you come to a T-junction, follow the minor road to the right — to a group of houses and the Hotel San Vicino (🏠). Past the hotel, turn left on a tarmac road which leads into the woods. Eventually this road runs to the west of Monte San Vicino (which can be easily climbed in about 30 minutes from the meadow at the highest point on the road). The road then descends along an open mountain ridge covered with sparse pastures, affording wonderful views across the Esino Valley and all the way to the Apennines (🗺).

*At the next sharp right-hand bend, turn left on the unsurfaced road to **Canfaito/Elcito**. After about 1km the tarmac starts, near a small stone monument. At this point two tracks lead right through a small wood to the meadows of Canfaito, with their large deciduous trees — a lovely place to picnic.*

You pass **Elcito** (🗺), a tiny depopulated village on a mountain spur and, beyond **Castel San Pietro** (🏠🅟), you reach the valley road. *Turn right and continue via **Palazzata** and **Cesolo** towards **San Severino**.*

The route now leads into welcoming open farmland with modest villages, where fields, orchards and, later, olive groves and small woods alternate. The high mountain ranges of the Monti Sibillini define the horizon in the south. Rough medieval defence towers dot the

*Above: Monte Catria, north of Cancelli;
right: San Cataldo (Walk 25)*

landscape, for instance near the
village of **Aliforni** (♣🏠) 5km south
of Castel San Pietro.

The pleasant provincial centre of
San Severino Marche★ (196km
i●♣M) also consists of a lively
lower town and an older upper
town that appears to be deserted.
From the oval main piazza in the
lower town a stepped path leads up
to the medieval *castello* and cathedral
(11-14C) — and also the Torre
Pendente, San Severino's own
'leaning tower'.

*Continue on the main road from San
Severino and follow the signposts
towards **Fabriano**, to pass through
Castelraimondo and Matelica.*
Beyond San Severino the route at
first runs along the narrow valley of
the Potenza. Near **Castelraimondo**
the valley widens. Driving through
fertile rolling country dotted with
old farmhouses you arrive in
Matelica (210km ▮M), which is
known for its good Verdicchio
white wine. In the historical centre,
where the rusty-red of the brick
dominates, you'll come upon some
lovely corners. The centre of the
small town is the lively Piazza
Enrico Mattei with the Palazzo

Pretorio and the adjacent arches of a
loggia.

At the southern entrance to the
village turn left on a country road
and follow this for 6km to the small
town of **Esanatoglia** (216km ●).
High on the slope above the
intricately-woven old centre stands
the little hermitage church of **San
Cataldo** (♣), which is the goal of
Walk 25. This church can also be
reached from the road to Collamato
but the final 200m from the start of
the Via Crucis (calvary) can only be
covered on foot.

Continue through rolling agricultural countryside with good views
(🎦). Beyond the friendly hill village

of **Collamato** you arrive in **San Michele**.

*Turn left here towards **Fabriano**. Cross the expressway and drive almost to the edge of the old town centre, then turn left towards **Rome** at the first traffic light and park.*

The historical centre of **Fabriano★** (234km *i*◉✝M) also merits a short walk. Most of the buildings, which were badly damaged in the 1997 earthquake, have now been restored. Apart from the central Piazza del Comune, framed by old façades, and various old churches, the paper museum (Museo della Carta) is especially interesting. Fabriano has been living from the manufacture of paper since the 13th century. The watermark for forgery-safe bank notes was developed here, and the first mechanical paper mill in Europe was operated on the Giano River.

*Beyond Fabriano keep on the old country road and ignore the approach to the Ancona/Rome highway. Once in Cancelli (▣), follow signposts to **Sassoferrato**, crossing the railway and expressway.*

The road leads through sparsely populated farmland, and wide-reaching cornfields and meadow slopes line the route. The main, steep-sided ridge of the Apennines rises in the west. Near **Melano** you pass a hill studded with a great many cypress trees. The landscape is harmonious and exciting at the same time.

*Joining the **Fabriano/Sassoferrato** road, follow it straight ahead for 250m and then turn left on the secondary road towards **Bastia/Rucce**. At the village of **Bastia**, by the bar/alimentari, turn left on a road which leads to Monte Cucco (not signposted).*

The tarmac ends on the edge of the small village of **Bastia** (▣). When you come to the next fork, bear right. This dirt road, easily motorable, curves up the slope of the ridge to Monte Cucco — all the

while with wonderful open views across the basin of Fabriano to Monte San Vicino (▣). Beyond the pass the road narrows considerably for some 500m (and is also quite bumpy). Then you join the tarmac road rising up from Sigillo and follow it to the right. Soon you reach a fork. The panoramic road straight ahead ends after 3km at a meadow (1200m; ▣), a very popular starting place for hang-gliders, while the turn-off to the right leads immediately to a woodland settlement in the Val di Ranco below **Monte Cucco** (261km ▲▲✕▣). You can go for wonderful walks in the Monte Cucco Nature Reserve (see Walks 21 and 22). There are thick beech woods, and in early summer the summit meadows are covered with wild flowers. Inside the mountain there is a vast network of caves — the fifth largest cave system on earth; naturally this is only accessible to experienced and well-equipped pot-holers.

*From Monte Cucco drive down the tarmac road to Sigillo, then follow the main road to the right past **Costacciaro**. Arriving at **Scheggia**, take the SS298 left towards **Gubbio**.* When you reach the lively small town of **Sigillo**, you will have finally left the Apennines behind. The road now leads through gently rolling Umbrian countryside. But beyond **Scheggia** and the Passo di Gubbio, the scenery becomes mountainous once more. The Canalecce stream flows through the short rocky valley of **Gola di Battaccione** (▣) between Monte Foce and Monte Ingino. Just where this valley starts, 2km before Gubbio, a short diversion on a side road branching off left leads to Coppo (▣⏞) and Sant'Ubaldo at Monte Ingino (✝□▲▲▣; Walk 15). At the end of the valley the town walls of medieval **Gubbio** (292km) suddenly appear before you.

Car tour 7: FROM URBINO THROUGH THE MONTEFELTRO

Urbino • Urbania • Sassocorvaro • San Leo • Pennabilli • Sant'Angelo in Vado • Piobbico • Furlo Gorge • Urbino

194km; 6-7 hours' driving. The roads are often narrow and winding, so progress will be slow. If you allow two days for this tour, I recommend staying overnight in picturesque San Leo.
Walks en route: 16, 17, 18
Picnic suggestions: from the free-standing bell-tower in tiny **Castello di Pietrarubbia** (52km) a path with benches leads up to the ruins of the Castello, from where you have good views of Monte Carpegna. • Near the village of **Pennabilli** (91km) you could climb either of two peaks — Penna or Billi — both of which have lovely places to stop, with good vantage points. To climb Billi, follow the yellow signpost for 'Castello', near the eastern entrance to the village. To get to Penna, with its Roccione viewpoint (benches), start

at the main piazza and follow Via Emanuele II (signposted to the *centro storico*). Pass the theatre on your right, then take the narrow lane Via delle Confraternite and turn left on Via Guasto, to climb the castle hill. • The rocky hill of **Mira-toio** (102km) also offers wonderful views, among others to the two table mountains of Simoncello and Sasso di Simone. From the village (opposite the well with a small stela), walk up a cobbled ramp for 20m, then follow signposted 'Walk 95' to the left around the mountain-side, past a small concrete building. You reach a wide path which leads to the peak in 5 minutes. • At the entrance to the **Gola di Furlo** (172km) there are lovely shady meadows near the Candigliano River.

The Montefeltro, the upland west of the famous Renaissance town of Urbino, is the destination of this circuit. With its furrowed valley slopes, bizarre cone-shaped mountains and seemingly isolated towns and villages, it seems a world away from nearby overcrowded Adriatic coast. This is a land for individualists, and with good reason the adopted home of poets like Umberto Eco, as well as film directors, painters and sculptors.

One of the focal points of the tour is small but spectacular San Leo, built against a steep rock face and a place of major cultural interest. We also come upon particularly beautiful countryside in the nature reserve of Sasso di Simone, at the foot of Monte Nerone, and around the short, but still impressive limestone gorge of Gola di Furlo (the latter outside the Montefeltro).

*Leave **Urbino** to the west on the road to **Urbania**.*
Beyond **Tufo** the route runs on breezy heights along a ridge, with far-reaching views west across the mountains of the Montefeltro and south to the Monte Catria massif (📷).
Urbania★ (16km 🍴🏛) is a small friendly town with an old historical centre. The most interesting sight is the Palazzo Ducale, situated above a loop of the river Metauro, another Renaissance building commissioned

by the Dukes of Montefeltro. It does not, however, quite measure up to the elegance and splendour of the main palace at Urbino. The mummified bodies exhibited in the Chiesa dei Morti are a rather morbid attraction.
*Return for 1km the way you came, towards Urbino, then turn left on the minor road uphill to **Peglio**, and, at the first houses, turn right towards **Sassocorvaro**.*
The road rises and, from a rest area (🏕) it is soon possible to get a good

San Leo Castle

view of the Metauro Valley and the small village of **Peglio** on a peak. The road from Peglio to Sasso-corvaro then leads into the rugged countryside of the **Montefeltro**. After driving through a valley you reach a long strung-out mountain ridge. At several points you have fine views out across valleys, settlements and small hillside churches to Monte Carpegna (1415m), the highest mountain in this region (☞). The distinctive table mountains of Sasso di Simone and Simoncello also come into view in the west. Then you arrive in the small village of **Sassocorvaro** (▮), hidden behind an elegant but robust Renaissance fortress.

Drive down into the valley of ***Mercatale****, situated on the shore of a small reservoir, turn off left on the valley road and, 1km past the village, take the right-hand fork towards* ***Carpegna****.*

Continue along a green river valley between wooded slopes and reach **Macerata Feltria** (●♣), where the road runs through the new lower town. On the northeastern slope above lies the small and deserted older district of Castello with the medieval town hall (Palazzo del

Podesta). Soon after Macerata Feltria the road towards Monte Carpegna climbs more steeply. On the left, reddish rocks appear, where you can see some old walls: these were part of the **Castello di Pietrarubbia** (52km ☐☞**M**). In **Mercato Vecchio** a small brown signpost directs you to an access road which leads to the village of Castello di Pietrarubbia; at one time this village was completely deserted, but today modern metal sculptures and other works of art are being exhibited there. A short footpath leads to the ridge with the castle ruin behind the village (see picnic suggestion).

About 2km beyond Mercato Vecchio you come to a group of houses called ***Ponte Cappuccini****, where you'll find the Visitors' Centre for the Riserva Naturale del Sasso di Simone. Turn right here, and continue towards* ***San Leo****.*

The road ascends the eastern side of Monte Carpegna, through barren countryside. Past the fairly new

Urbino

holiday resort of **Villagrande** at the
foot of an isolated rocky peak, you
crest a pass with distant views of the
Adriatic coast (🏠🖼). The road
then descends to a fork in front of
the pilgrimage church of Madonna
di Pugliano, where you turn right. A
short while later the impressive
fortress of San Leo comes into view
— a massive castle high on the top
of a sheer-sided mountain ridge
(🖼). You reach the village of **San
Leo**★ (72km *i*●✝🛏) via a narrow
single-lane access road leading
round the rock. Driving through the
town gate you immediately find
yourself in the pleasant little Piazza
Dante. (Continue straight on to the
car park just below the *centro
storico*.) From the piazza make your
way up to the terraces around the
castle, from where you will have an
incredible panoramic view (🖼). Be
sure to visit San Leo's cathedral and
the even older, well-preserved
medieval church buildings of the
Pieve Santa Maria.
*Return from San Leo the way you came
until, 1km before* **Villagrande**, *you
can turn right on the minor road
towards* **Soanne**.
The road descends in curves along
the northern slopes of Monte
Carpegna, with views across the
valley of the Marecchia (🖼). Small
meadows offer good places to take a
break amidst this harmonious
countryside.
In **Soanne** *bear left towards* **Maciano**,
then, 1km past the little village of
Cernitosa, *turn left again on the road
to* **Scavolino**.
You drive through sparsely
populated highlands, via the remote
village of **Scavolino**, then come into
Pennabilli★ (91km ●▯), named
after two destroyed Malatesta castles
— Penna and Billi — between
which the small village centre lies.
The two rocky hills, Rupe and
Roccione, on which these two
castles once stood, are easily climbed
and are worth the effort for the

good views (see picnic suggestion).
In the village follow signposts to **Ponte
Messa/Sansepolcro** *and, 1km below
Pennabilli, turn left towards*
Carpegna/Miratoio.
You drive through a valley, then
wind uphill to a pass with far-
reaching views (🖼). Forking right,
descend with more fine views, to
Miratoio (103km), from where
Walk 16 leads to Sasso di Simone.
The few houses of this village nestle
below a rock face. The road towards
Sestino now leads through beautiful
Apennine countryside with large
meadows and lonely woodlands.
Beyond **Petrella**, at a pass, you can
look back towards the bizarre twin
peaks of **Simoncello** and **Sasso di
Simone** — isolated rocky plateaus
facing each other (🖼). The narrow
road then descends steeply past
eroded valley furrows to **Sestino**
(112km) in the Foglio Valley.
*Turn right in Sestino, cross the river
Foglio, then follow a narrow winding
road (unsurfaced for 3km). Cross the
Passo della Spugna and descend into
the valley of Borgo Pace, where the
Meta and Auro streams meet to become
the Metauro, then turn left on the
SS73.*
This well-built trunk road follows
the course of the **Metauro River**
through a more central European
landscape, with deciduous forests,
small streams and green meadows.
Soon the few houses of semi-
deserted **Castello della Pieve**
appear up on the slopes to the left.
It is worthwhile stopping briefly in
the next village, **Mercatello sul
Metauro** (●✝🛏M), to look around
the small historical centre by the
Piazza Garibaldi, with the Palazzo
Comunale and the Chiesa San
Francesco (which houses an art
gallery).
The next, larger town of
Sant'Angelo in Vado (133km ●🛏),
7km downhill, is surrounded by
new buildings and small factories.
At first glance you would not guess

Piobbico Castle

that it still has an undamaged historical centre. The focus of the medieval town was the Piazza Pio with the town hall (Palazzo della Ragione), today a quiet place. Nowadays people gather at the Piazza Garibaldi on the southern shore of the river, with its bars and street cafes.

In Sant'Angelo in Vado turn right across the Metauro, leaving the SS73 and making for Piobbico. Then, on the edge of town, do not miss the left fork for Piobbico.

Again on a little-used road, you ascend a wooded valley with few houses to the mountain saddle between the Metauro and Candigliano valleys. From here you look across green meadows — covered with wildflowers in early summer — to the massif of Monte Nerone (📷).

Some lovely walks can be taken near **Piobbico** (150km ⬛⬛), at the confluence of the Biscubio and the Candigliano (see Walk 18). The only place of interest in this remote small town is the old district of Castello near the Candigliano, with the Rocca, the well-preserved castle of the medieval Brancaleoni dynasty.

Continue on the SS257 to Acqualagna, where you ignore the signposts to the Fano/Rome highway. Drive into the village, then turn left on the old country road to Fossombrone. At the edge of the village follow the yellow signs to Furlo.

East of Piobbico the valley road continues between steep rocks along the winding Candigliano river for several kilometres, then follows the river valley as it widens into the typical rolling farmland of the Marche. **Acqualagna** is of little interest, although it does claim to be 'Italy's truffle capital'. Once a year in autumn the small town comes alive for the large truffle fair.

Beyond **San Vicenzo al Furlo**

(171km ⬛⬛⬛), a Romanesque church near a grassy rest area to the right of the road, the character of the landscape once more becomes dramatic. Near the hamlet of **Furlo** (172km) steep limestone rocks rise above the turquoise waters of the Candigliano and form the short but impressive **Gola di Furlo★** (Walk 17). The old road through the gorge has been closed to motor traffic. So you have to take a little walk to enjoy the dramatic scenery at leisure. At the end of the gorge, about 2.5km from Furlo hamlet, the road leads through a well-preserved Roman tunnel — part of the ancient Via Flaminia.

From Furlo hamlet follow the signs for Fano to join the expressway coming from Rome. It crosses the mountains to the north of the Gola di Furlo via a tunnel. About 4km after leaving the tunnel change to the SS73 bis to Urbino, another expressway, which soon narrows to a two-lane road.

Driving through a quiet woodland landscape and past the large viaduct of a defunct railway line, you arrive back in **Urbino** (194km).

Car tour 8: ASCOLI PICENO AND THE MONTI SIBILLINI

Ascoli Piceno • Foce • Amandola • Sarnano • Lago di Fiastra • Visso •
Piano Grande di Castelluccio • Acquasanta Terme • Ascoli Piceno •
Montagna dei Fiori • Ascoli Piceno

246km, 7-8 hours' driving; a two-day tour, often on narrow and winding secondary roads. Good places to stay overnight include the lovely little town of Sarnano and the isolated Altopiano di Castelluccio. From December till March be prepared for snow on the passes of Forca di Gualdo (1496m) and Forca di Presta (1536m).

Walks en route: 26, 27, 29-36
Picnic suggestions: There are many places to picnic in the untouched countryside of the Monti Sibillini. An early choice is at the western end of **Lago di Gerosa** (34km), in a shady meadow in front of the Romanesque village church of San Giorgio all'Isola, at the left of the road. • If you drive through the village of **Foce** (44km) to the end of the tarmac road, you will find shaded picnic spots near the stream.

• There are good places all around the **Santuario Madonna dell' Ambro** near Montefortino (70km), alongside the Ambro, but expect crowds at weekends. • Not far past the dam wall near **Lago di Fiastra** (110km) a path on the right leads to the blue waters of this lovely lake, where you can picnic on the shore. • The meadows and stone benches inside the circular wall of the **Santuario Madonna di Macereto** (128km) were used as resting and camping places by pilgrims back in the 16th century. • All around the **plateau of Castelluccio** (166km) there are lovely picnic spots on the grassy slopes, but little shade. • The meadows of **Colle San Marco** (222km) in the mountains south of Ascoli Piceno are very popular with the Ascolanis themselves.

In the southern Marche, on the border with Umbria, the Apennines look very Alpine in places. Here you find the Monti Sibillini, the scenic highlight of this guide, with their steep rock faces, many round grassy peaks, remote plateaus and deep gorges. These mountains, which rise to almost 2400m, have always been a land of myths and legends. Even today some inhabitants are convinced that Sibylle, a powerful witch, lives in a grotto deep in the mountain, and that high in the mountains near Lago di Pilato (where Pontius Pilate is supposed to have drowned) evil mountain spirits are still casting spells.

There are simply wonderful walks through the remote Sibillini. This car tour opens up the most beautiful areas of the range and leads to the starting points of ten walks. One of the best times to be here is early summer, when the flowering poppies on the plateau of Castelluccio are an exceptional sight.

The starting- and end-point of the tour, Ascoli Piceno in the Tronto Valley, is an impressive old town with a picturesque piazza and 16 Romanesque churches. Although it lies outside the Sibillini, its gates open out to two other mountain ranges — the Monti della Laga and Montagna dei Fiori, on the border with Abruzzi. Here, too, you find untouched countryside and more possibilities for walks through beech and chestnut forests, to waterfalls and mountain pastures.

Sarnano (above) and Lago di Gerosa

Leave **Ascoli Piceno** to the west and follow the main road towards **Rome** as far as the edge of town. Then turn right on the expressway towards **San Benedetto**. This takes you round the north side of Ascoli Piceno. Once over the Tronto bridge, take the right fork to **Venarotta/Palmiano**, crossing over the expressway.

This quiet secondary road winds uphill through friendly rolling countryside with views to the steep westerly slopes of Monte Ascensione (📷). In **Venarotta** (🍴) bear left, to drive down into the valley of Roccafluvione.

Once in the valley, take the main SS78 road to the right towards **Amandola**. The road ascends more steeply as you pass the turn-off to Montegallo. Soon steep-sided Monte Vettore, nearly 2500m high, appears in the west above the thickly wooded peaks of the foothills (📷).

10km north of Roccafluvione, at a pass near the hamlet of **Calvarese**, *turn left on the secondary road towards* **Polverina**; *after 3km bear right downhill and drive via* **Gerosa** *to the valley road; turn left towards the mountains.* You pass old farmsteads and arrive in the valley of the Aso, which was dammed to form the **Lago di Gerosa**. From a car park at the start of the lake a short path leads down to the shore, where the dark silhouette of the Monti Sibillini is mirrored in the clear turquoise-blue waters (📷). The official bathing

ban does not deter the locals from taking a dip in these cool waters! At the entrance to **San Giorgio all'Isola** (🧍) at the western end of the lake, the little Romanesque village church with interesting frescoes stands at the left of the road, but is nearly always closed. *At the fork past the village continue left towards* **Montegallo**; *2km further on, take the access road right into the valley of* **Foce**.

This detour leads straight into the centre of the untouched Monti Sibillini. The road penetrates the valley of the young Aso, through steep-sided mountains. Once past the group of houses called **Rocca**, the valley narrows into a rocky

41

gorge (⌖). You come to the little village of **Foce** (44km) at the foot of high mountains — and seem to have arrived at the end of the world. Past the last houses the valley road continues as a footpath, rising high into the mountains — to the legendary Lago di Pilato.

From Foce retrace your route for 5km, then turn left and drive uphill along a winding road towards **Montemonaco**. The modest tourist village of **Montemonaco** (⌖ ▲ ✕ ⌖) is situated along a ridge at almost 1000m. The village enjoys wonderful views, and a castle ruin towers above it.

At the eastern end of this village, leave the trunk road to Amandola by forking left on a minor road. This runs through wonderful mountain scenery via **Isola San Biagio** *and the turn-off to Rubbiano, back to the main road. Immediately below Montefortino, fork left on the access road to* **Madonna dell'Ambro**.

From Rubbiano a dirt track leads west to the start of Walk 32 which explores the wild **Infernaccio Gorge**. Walk 31 — a tough hike — begins near **Madonna dell'Ambro** (⌖ ▪ ⌖), a place of pilgrimage next to a roaring stream. **Montefortino** (⌖ ⌖) is a pretty village with old lanes stretching picturesquely uphill towards the church, which stands out against a backdrop of high mountains.

From Montefortino continue on the SS78 via **Amandola** *to* **Sarnano**. **Amandola** (81km ⌖ ▲ ▪ ⌖) is a comparatively lively town on the edge of the mountains. From the piazza lanes run uphill past old brick façades to the Teatro Fenica, from where you can see across the roof-tops of Amandola to Monte Vettore. The onward road to Sarnano leads straight through the middle of Amandola's main piazza to a small town gate — sometimes leading to typically Italian, chaotic traffic. The tour continues with good views

east across landscape typical of the Marche — hills both round and furrowed, with meadows and cornfields — and west to the steep slopes of the Monti Sibillini. Suddenly, as you round a right-hand bend, **Sarnano★** (93km *i* ⌖ ▲ ▪ ⌖) comes into view, the houses of the old town huddled against a steep hill. I do not recommend trying to take your car into the narrow *centro storico*. A stepped path, the 13th-century Via della Costa, leads up to the Piazza Alta, with its three medieval town hall buildings and the Chiesa Santa Maria Assunta (also 13th century), where there are several interesting paintings.

Drive for 6km towards **Macerata** *on the main SS78 road, then turn left towards* **Tolentino**. *1km further on turn left again on the secondary road to* **Fiastra**.

The winding road to Fiastra leads back into a sparsely populated mountain landscape. Beyond the hamlet of **Monastero** (106km), the rugged landscape of the **Gola del Fiastrone★** appears on the left. Roadside scrub obscures the view into the gorge, but Walk 26 would let you explore this rocky, steep-sided valley with its hermitage grottos on foot.

After the slightly dark gorge passage, the tour continues along the shore of **Lago di Fiastra★** (⌖), a turquoise-blue lake framed by barren mountains. You can swim at the western end, away from the dam, but even in summer the water is fairly cold, as the lake is fed by mountain streams.

In the small tourist village of **San Lorenzo al Lago** *take the road towards* **Visso**; *this climbs southwest across a spur of the lake, with views to the mountains. 4km from San Lorenzo, past the houses of* **Colle**, *turn left on a minor road. After a further 3km (and before reaching Sant'Ilario), go left for* **Visso, Cupi, Macereto**.

A narrow, little-used tarmac road

now continues along the western side of the mountains. Again and again you enjoy far-reaching views across the Monti Sibillini, which now present themselves from a new perspective. Unlike the eastern side, the west reveals round grassy ridges sloping gently down towards Umbria.

Past the farm village of **Cupi** the church **Madonna di Macereto★** (✝) comes into view. This remote Renaissance building was built in the 16th century near the pilgrimage route from Rome to the sanctuary of Loreto, to protect travellers from wolves and bandits. A wall encircles the symmetrical central building; the elegant ensemble somehow looks out of place up here in these lonely mountains.

Just before the church, turn left on an unmarked minor road.

The route again gains height as it runs alongside wide mountain meadows. The impressive rocky pyramid of Monte Bove (2112m) appears ahead and, from a flat saddle you enjoy a lovely panorama of the steep northern side of the mountain (📷). From here the road descends to a fork, where you go straight on towards Casali. At the next fork bear right downhill towards Ussita. (The left fork leads to Casali, starting point for Walk 30.) From **Ussita** (🏔▣), a small tourist village, continue through green wooded mountains on the valley road beside the Torrente Ussita to **Visso★** (142km ●✝🏔✕▣), a friendly little town with a lovely old piazza.

West of the central piazza turn left and keep following signposts towards Castelluccio.

The road first runs through the deeply furrowed forest valley of the young Nera, which rises near the tightly clustered mountain village of **Castelsantangelo** (●). The road ascends in twists and turns, with an ever-widening mountain panorama.

Pass the turn-off to the mountain village of Gualdo and climb to a pass, the **Forca di Gualdo** (1496m). Beyond the pass, the **Piano Grande di Castelluccio★** unexpectedly reveals itself (📷): a wide, empty landscape with bizarre features which one hardly associated with central Italy. On a hill above the plain are the few houses of **Castelluccio** (166km 🏔✕▣), the highest permanently inhabited settlement in the Apennines. Walks 27 and 29 begin here.

From Castelluccio the route leads 2km down into the wide Piano Grande, at which point you turn left uphill towards Ascoli Piceno.

With views across the plain, where lentil fields and cornfields draw geometric patterns (📷), you reach the **Forca di Presta** (1534m), the highest point in our circuit round the Sibillini. The road then descends below the steep southern side of Monte Vettore towards Arquata del Tronto. From the strange 'south American' landscape of the high plateau you arrive in a more familiar mountain region with pine and larch woods. At several points you enjoy

good views across the Tronto Valley to the Monti della Laga and Abruzzi (☎).

Beyond **Pretare** you come into **Arquata del Tronto** (182km ●▮▆), a quiet old hill village. Above the houses the Rocca dating back to the 12th century stands guard; from the castle tower you have another good view of the mountain world.

Meeting the main SS4 road, the Via Salaria, in the lower part of Trisungo, head back towards Ascoli Piceno.

The landscape changes once again in the Tronto Valley. Thick beech and chestnut woods, interspersed with smooth rock walls, now cover the northern side of Macera della Morte (2073m) in the Monti della Laga. This little-explored mountain area on the border of the Marche, Lazio and Abruzzi is among the most sparsely inhabited regions of Italy.

Past the old village of **Quinto-decimo** (●), built on a hill above the river, and a narrow access road off right to Umito, where Walk 33 begins, you reach the spa village of **Acquasanta Terme** (194km ▲▲✕), where the air smells of sulphur.

Now take the Via Salaria, which continues to follow the course of the Tronto, to drive back through calm rolling countryside to Ascoli Piceno.

From **Ascoli Piceno** (214km) it's possible to tack on a short circuit through the highlands of **Montagna dei Fiori**, which lies largely in Abruzzi. The spurs of the 'Flower Mountain', which rises to some 1800m, begin just at the edge of town. The popular tourist destination of Ascolani offers wonderful natural landscapes and possibilities for good walks.

Leave the centre of Ascoli Piceno near the cathedral square, going east on the Corso Emanuele. Beyond the Tronto bridge, opposite the station, turn right on the Viale Marconi. At the following traffic light carry straight on towards Colle San Marco.

The road snakes steadily uphill between olive groves and oleanders. Walk 34, to the monastery of San Marco, begins in the village of **Piagge**. Some 4km further on, near the scattered houses of **Colle San Marco** (♦⌂), meadows and small woods stretch out along the road-side; on Sundays these are popular picnic places. The road then continues to gain height as it leads through dark pines and fir trees.

Below **San Giacomo** (230km) a panorama opens up to the west — to the Monti della Laga and Monti Sibillini. A *caciare* stands in a meadow at the right of the road — an ancient drystone cottage reminiscent of the *trullis* in Murgia or the *bories* in Provence (☎). This tourist village (▲▲✕▮), with its simple buildings, is near the starting point for Walk 35 to Monte Girella (1814m), while Walk 36 into the Salinello Gorge begins near Ripe, 9km to the southeast.

In San Giacomo turn right towards San Vito, where you again bear right and zig-zag all the way down to the Castellano Valley.

On the valley road turn right and skirt the Torrento Castellano as you drive back to Ascoli Piceno. Along the way you could stop at small **Castel Trosino** (●▮), a restored medieval village rising picturesquely on an isolated rocky ridge. At the end of the 19th century a Longo-bard necropolis containing valuable relics was discovered near the village; some are now exhibited in the archaeological museum at **Ascoli Piceno** (246km).

Walking

Until a few decades ago, walking as a leisure activity was largely unknown in Italy outside the nature reserves in the Alps and Abruzzi. But gradually a change of attitude seems to have taken place. All over the country, the local people have started to explore the scenic beauty of their native country on foot, and in many places hiking routes have been waymarked and signposted, while local branches of the national hiking club CAI (Club Alpino Italiano) have sprung up. But the landscapes explored in this guide are much less frequented than those in the long-popular Alps and on the Mediterranean islands.

Maps, waymarks, GPS

Good **maps** are not yet available for all areas of Italy, so walking in Umbria and the Marche is still a bit of a foray into the unknown. Nor is **waymarking** 100% reliable: sometimes marks fade out in the middle of a walk, suddenly to reappear later, or the colouring/style of waymarking may change en route for no obvious reason. The bold red lines on the maps that *are* available, which *should* indicate waymarked, well-established routes, often turn out to be small paths thickly overgrown with macchia.

For this reason I have tried to make the descriptions of the walks in this book so comprehensive that you should be able to find your way even *without* waymarks. Also bear in mind that some of my walks only follow *part* of a waymarked route, so *always* refer to the text. Waymarks on the ground at the time of writing are mentioned, but I cannot guarantee that they will still be there in two or three years' time! For those of you who use **GPS**, free **track** downloads are available for all the walks; see the Umbria/Marche page on the Sunflower Books website.

All Italy has been mapped by the Istituto Geografico Militare (IGM) at a scale of 1:50,000 or 1:25,000. But in general these sheets are only reliable for topography. In most cases the routes — whether tracks, trails or paths — are no longer up to date (some maps are still reporting the situation on the ground in 1953!). Even though the IGM has started to revise all the sheets, outside the high mountain areas (where the old trails mostly still exist) you cannot easily navigate with these maps in open terrain. So it is questionable whether it's worth buying any of them; moreover you'll hardly ever see them for sale outside the cities.

Maps in the 1;25,000 'Carta dei Sentieri' series, published by the CAI, are more reliable, but they only cover certain areas.

Where a good map for a walk exists, I mention it in the introductory text. But the maps in this book, together with the walking notes, should be sufficient for route-finding.

When to walk

In the lower mountain ranges, spring (from April to mid-June) and autumn (mid-September to the end of October) are the best seasons for walking. Temperatures are pleasant and often a clear blue sky arches above the undulating hills. But be prepared for rain every now and then, especially from April to mid-May and in October, although in general wet conditions will not last very long. During high summer it's often *very* hot: only by starting at sunrise, to be back home by noon at the latest, can a walk be enjoyed.

It's also pleasant to walk from November to March, at least in the lower areas, if the weather (rather unpredictable during this period) is kind to you. Sometimes it rains for days on end; sometimes there are spells of warm sunny weather, and sometimes temperatures drops below zero with no clouds at all and fantastic far-reaching views.

On the **high mountains** of the Apennines, especially in the Monti Sibillini, conditions are of course a bit different. You can even hike here in high summer, while in winter deep snow often covers the ground. The scenery up here is especially beautiful in early summer, when millions of wild flowers are in bloom.

Equipment

No special equipment is necessary for any of the walks in this book, but good **walking boots** with sturdy soles are highly recommended: many routes lead across stony and sometimes sloping terrain, where you need good ankle protection. Especially in the high Apennines you always should have a **waterproof** and extra clothing with you, as sudden unpredictable changes in the weather must be taken into account.

From May to October always take **sun protection** (headgear, suncream, sunglasses); several routes have long sections in full sun. Most of the walks offer no chance for refreshment en route. So take enough **food** and, *even more important, plenty of drinking water* (at least 1.5 litres for a whole day, 2.5 litres in summer) in a refillable container; some walks pass springs or fountains with drinking water *(acqua potabile)*. On warm days, when there are long ascents en route, the requirement for water is *very high*.

All year round you should take a small **first aid kid**, a knife, a whistle, extra socks and shoelaces and warm clothing. Long trousers and a shirt with long sleeves protect against sunburn and thorny plants. A walking stick can be very useful; it lessens the wear on your ankles and knees and gives support on tricky descents, when fords have to be crossed, and when obstacles, undergrowth or unfriendly dogs block the route.

Walk descriptions, grading

The spectrum of walks in this book ranges from **simple rambles** through the rolling hills of Umbria to long, **fairly demanding hikes** in the Monti Sibillini (which, nevertheless, do not require any mountaineering skills). With the exception of Walk 11, this guide only includes half-day and full-day walks.

The walks are **graded** for walkers with an average physical fitness. A walking speed of 4km/h on flat terrain and an ascent of 350m per hour are taken as a basis. **Times** shown are *neat walking times*. When planning your walk, be sure to increase walking times by *at least* a third, to allow for rest breaks, taking pictures and sightseeing.

In Italy walking is considered pure sport: that's why even on some of the main, waymarked hiking routes you may come upon 'delicate' passages (sloping rocks, steep stony descents, narrow exposed paths besides precipices, etc). While none of these is an insurmountable obstacle to the average hiker, *those lacking a head for heights or who are less sure-footed and agile on stony sloping ground should read the full description of the walk in advance, to be prepared for possible difficulties.*

Most of the routes are designed as circuits for motorists (although some may be accessible by bus/train), but a few are linear and require using public transport. Except for two walks, my linear routes also offer a variation that can be done as a circuit. Where required, I give details of bus/train schedules (valid at the time of writing). Of course timetables can change at any time. Fewer buses run during school holidays (mid-June to mid-September, one week around Easter, two weeks around Christmas) and on Saturdays; hardly any run on Sundays.

Safety and precautions

Some walks, especially those through the mountains of the Apennines, cross very remote areas. Outside the high summer holiday season and weekends you often are alone on the tracks and trails and won't meet another soul for hours. That is why it is always advisable **not to walk alone**. *Always* inform a reliable person where you are going and when you expect to be back.

Some hikes run across high mountains. The Monti Sibillini and the Monti della Laga, as well as the high ridges of the Apennines in Umbria and the Marche have a reputation for sudden changes in weather. At noon thick clouds may come up quickly and **heavy thunderstorms** break out. Before starting out, *check the weather forecast carefully* and en route look early for a shelter or escape route back to base if a thunderstorm gathers.

In open country farms and villas are often guarded by **watchdogs**, most of them chained up. Exceptions may occur, so it is best to approach these places with caution. You may feel more comfortable with an anti-dog pepper spray or an ultrasound device (a 'Dog Dazer', available from sunflowerbooks.co.uk).

Every now and then herds of goats and sheep are encountered en route. Because of the **guard dogs**, keep your distance if the herdsman is not around, and wait to let the animals pass before continuing. Groups of **half-wild horses** or **grazing cows** roam freely in the Apennines. I have always found them peaceful, *but* it is best to keep a little distance here also, so as not to disturb the animals — especially if foals or calves are within the herds.

Most of the **snakes** you may see are harmless, especially the Aesculapian serpent (pictured on medical symbols; it can be up to 2m long). But **poisonous vipers** *(Vipera aspis)* do occur — small brownish-grey snakes with dark horizontal stripes and a triangular head. They have a wide distribution area throughout the Mediterranean, but are infrequently seen. Generally they only bite if threatened. If you are bitten, keep calm and get medical aid as quickly as possible. For the normally fit person a bite should not be lethal. But because of vipers, always wear sturdy shoes *(never sandals)*, and take care when you sit down — especially on stony ground, by walls, in meadows and near damp places.

Outside winter **stinging insects** can be annoying. Keep clear of **beehives** near the walking route. Blood-sucking **ticks**, the bites of which may spread dangerous disease, live in the deciduous woods of the Apennines among other places. When showering after a walk, look carefully to see if one has fixed itself to your skin. If so, remove it quickly with tweezers or see a doctor.

The passion for hunting in rural Italy is a real nuisance. The **hunting season** begins in autumn (exact timings in different areas must be checked locally). Especially at weekends, take care when walking in open country. *Do not leave the route* and, if hunters are near, *draw attention to yourself* by shouting loudly.

Below is a key to the symbols on the walking maps:

Symbol	Description	Symbol	Description	Symbol	Description
	dual carriageway	spring, fountain, etc		castle, fort.ruins
	trunk road	church, monastery		prehistoric site
	secondary road	chapel		cave.quarry
	minor road	cross, shrine		campsite
	motorable track	signpost for walkers		building.in ruins
	other track or trail	cemetery		refuge.monument
	footpath, steps	picnic site		agriturismo
2→	main walk	viewpoint		transmitter, mast
2→	alternative walk	bus stop		rockface, cliff
400	height in metres	railway station		tower.mill
		car parking		electricity substation

Walk 1: PASSIGNANO, LAKE TRASIMENO AND ISOLA MAGGIORE

Distance/time: 10km; 3h45min
Grade: easy, overall ascent of 350m; mostly good tracks and trails. Follow the notes carefully on the initial ascent to the ridge (few waymarks).
Equipment: as pages 46-47; good shoes are sufficient
Refreshments: bars and a restaurant on Isola Maggiore
How to get there: 🚌 to Passignano

(Car tour 1 at the 30km-point) or 🚂 (Perugia/Terontola line; one train per hour during the week, on Sundays every two hours).
Note: on weekends and from mid-June to mid-September Maggiore Island is likely to be very crowded.
Short walks: Passignano circuit (easy, 7km, 2h45min) or island circuit (very easy, 3km, 1h)

From the little town of Passignano, a pleasant holiday resort on the northern shores of Lake Trasimeno, the first circuit of this walk climbs through olive groves, broom meadows and small woods to a ridge. Looking back down from here, the wide blue lake, dotted with three tiny islands, is laid out before you. Back at Passignano, we take the ferry to nearby Isola Maggiore, an unspoilt idyllic islet without any road traffic and only one tiny village, which we discover on the second circuit of the walk.

Start the walk at Piazza Trento e Trieste in **Passignano**. Opposite the town hall (Municipio) climb steps at the right of the tourist office and go through an archway into the small *centro storico*. Immediately behind the gate take the stepped lane rising to the left. (A short detour straight on would take you to Piazza Castello with a beautiful view over the lake.) Turn left through a second archway to leave the medieval town centre. Beyond the village walls, follow the small road Via della Rocca uphill, in five minutes coming to a crossroads (**10min**). Continue slightly right uphill on the wide earthen track lined by olive trees (⌐: Sentiero M25, red/

white waymarks). At the next crossroads go straight ahead through cypresses to **Villa le Masse** with its little church (**25min**).
Pass to the right of the villa, following a shady path slightly downhill. It veers right through a small valley. In just under 10 minutes you come to a fork: turn left on a clear path, rising alongside olive groves. In a good five minutes you arrive at the few houses of **Cerqueto**, where you meet a small road (**40min**). Follow this a short way uphill beyond the uppermost house, where the tarmac ends. At the left-hand bend 50m further on, take the path continuing straight ahead, rising slightly between oak

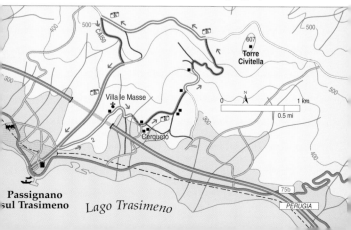

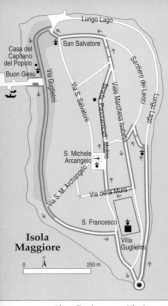

Isola Maggiore

0   N   250 m

Above Passignano, with views over Lake Trasimeno

trees. Some five minutes from Cerqueto you're on an open grassy slope, blanketed with yellow-blooming broom in May and June and offering far-reaching views to Lake Trasimeno. Veering left, the path joins a track. After passing through a hollow the cypress-lined track brings you to an **old stone villa** within five minutes. Pass to the right of the villa and join a major track (**55min**). Follow this track, winding uphill for about 15 minutes to an **old stone house** overlooking these rolling hills (**1h10min**). Pass to the right of the building and continue straight ahead uphill on a small track. At the Y-fork some 150m above the old stone house go right (red/white waymarks); at another Y-fork three minutes later, go right again. You are now on an old trail, which leads through typical Mediterranean forest with many cypresses. It climbs the hill, initially heading northeast for about 10 minutes, then veers left (northwest). Strawberry bushes grow beside the trail; in autumn they are full of little red and yellow fruits — edible, but

not very tasty. Steadily climbing, you reach the **main ridge** (**1h40min**) on the north side of **Lake Trasimeno**. From here you overlook a large expanse of lake, with little Polvese Island. A line of cypresses makes a nice foreground, and a small meadow a pleasant picnic spot. A wide track runs along the top of this main ridge; follow it to the left (west) for about 20 minutes. At first it climbs a short way, then descends with views towards the islands in Lake Trasimeno and the extensive wooded hills of the hinterland. As you approach an old stone house, ignore a track descending to the left; keep to the ridge for three more minutes. Then, 50m behind a little pond at the left of the main track, and just before a stand of dark pines, turn sharp left on a trail (**2h**; red and white waymarks of the CAI50). This descends for about 10 minutes through broom-macchia and with views down to the lake, then meets a small surfaced road. Follow this straight ahead downhill, with blue Lake Trasimeno laid out before you. On the edge of **Passignano** you

come back to the crossroads encountered earlier and follow your outgoing route back to the Piazza Trento e Trieste. Walk 150m left, to the **jetty** (**2h45min**) for the ferry trip to **Isola Maggiore**.

Start the walk on the island from the **landing stage**: walk the few steps to Via Guglielmi, the single lane of the island's tiny village, with about 50 year-round inhabitants. In front of the houses the older women sit in the sun, producing traditional fine embroidery and having a natter. Follow Via Guglielmi to the right and, when it ends, take the ongoing, gently climbing track. Veering left above the southern shore, it leads to the walls of the ruined, castle-like **Villa Guglielmi**, built around a medieval Franciscan monastery at the end of the 19th century by the wealthy Guglielmis. Once the meeting place of 'beautiful people', it was looted in 1960 and left to decay (but plans are afoot to restore it).

Some 50m in front of the villa take a path down to the right. This leads to the **base of a ruined windmill** at the southernmost point of the island,

a pleasant picnic spot. Walking north from here on a flat trail beside the shore, five minutes brings you to a chapel with a **statue of Saint Francis**, commemorating the saint's 40 days' fast at this spot. Walk 30m past the statue, then take a stepped trail up the slope to the left. At a fork, go left, back to the Villa Guglielmi enclosure. Veering right, you approach the church of **San Michele Arcangelo**, standing on the island's highest point. The plain 14th-century building houses interesting frescoes (14th-16th century) and a painted cross (15th century).

Continue on the trail, to the right of the church (⌐: 'Strada Panoramica di Mulino'). You pass the base of a Roman tower and come to the 12th-century **Chiesa San Salvatore** (usually closed) and the **Albergo-Ristorante** Da Sauro beyond it. The island's short sandy beach begins at the right of the restaurant. Follow the lane 150m to the left, past the medieval **Casa del Capitano del Popolo** (Chief of Police), to return to the **landing stage** (**3h45min**).

Walk 2: MONTE TEZIO DI PERUGIA

Distance/time: 10km, 3h15min
Grade: moderate, with an overall
ascent/descent of 550m, mostly on
good tracks and paths; occasional
waymarks and signposts; little shade
Equipment: as pages 46-47; sun
and rain protection
Refreshments: none en route
How to get there: 🚗 see Car tour 1

from Perugia to Cenerente (the
5km-point), where you turn right on
the minor road to Migiana di Monte
Tezio (which eventually becomes
unsurfaced). Leave the car on the
bend to the right, 50m before
reaching the hamlet. No public
transport.

I solated Monte Tezio (961m), north of Perugia, offers wide-
ranging views. Below the treeless summit with its extensive
meadows, the unending green and undulating hills of central
Umbria are at your feet. The bright surface of Lake Trasimeno
shines through the haze to the west while, to the east, the dark
ranges of the Apennines border the horizon.

Start the walk in **Migiana di
Monte Tezio** (530m). At the right-
hand bend 50m in front of the
hamlet, take the track straight ahead
(red/white waymarks). This climbs
to the left of the first houses,
towards **Castello Procoio**, a luxury
hotel (www.santaeurasia.it) which
soon comes into view. Then it dips
50m, to a bend to the right. Here
you leave the main track to nearby
Procoio Castle, instead taking a
grassy path branching off to the left
(**10min**). The path leads through
wild rose bushes and shrubs. In just
three minutes you come to a spring
with a trough, where you turn left.
The path rises southwest up slopes
thick with broom, gorse and scrub.

Eventually you reach a promontory
with a wooden cross, **Croce Fontenova** (712m; **30min**), offering a
good view over Migiana di Monte
Tezio and down to the valley of the
river Tiber.
At the junction 30m above the cross,
take the flat path to the left, which
contours the hillside (➤: Sentiero
Marcaccioli; red/white waymarks of
the CAI5). Veering to the right, you
pass through a conifer wood and
meet a track. Go right here, slightly
uphill, to the **Belvedere** (**55min**), a
viewpoint with benches and wide
panoramic views.
From here the track descends along
the dry southern slopes of Monte
Tezio, where holm oaks and

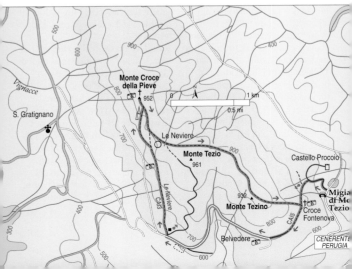

Above: the Palazzo dei Priori and Fontana Maggiore in Perugia; right: Castello Procoio, before conversion to a lxury hotel

cypresses grow. After a track joins from the left, the route contours and runs alongside the fence of a wolves' preserve. Beyond the enclosure you come to a signposted crossroads by a **stone hut** (650m; **1h15min**). Take the path climbing to the left of the building (■: Le Neviere; CAI3). It keeps gaining height along the western slopes of Tezio. Initially you're walking in the shade of pine trees and cypresses, later the forest thins out and you catch glimpses of Lake Trasimeno in the west. After curving to the right and then to the left, you enter a meadow with junipers and young conifers. Behind a derelict fence the path forks. The more-worn branch goes right along the ridge, but you follow instead the smaller path straight ahead alongside the fence, through some bushes. A short climb at the left of some rocky outcrops brings you to the summit cross, **Croce della Pieve** (952m; **2h**), from where you enjoy a splendid panoramic view. From the cross continue south along the wide grassy mountain ridge. Five minutes from Croce della Pieve you pass to the left of a hollow with bushes, called **le Neviere**. Ice cubes were once stored here and sold in the markets at Perugia.

Just before the flat summit ridge of **Monte Tezio** (961m), turn left and follow a grassy trail east through a hollow, to **Monte Tezino** (932m; **2h25min**). Walk to the left of the small transmitter here and follow a small path (with occasional red and white waymarks) straight ahead in the same easterly direction, now descending more steeply. You come back to the fork above **Croce Fontenova** (**2h50min**), from where you follow your outgoing route back to **Migiana di Monte Tezio** (**3h15min**).

Walk 3: CIRCUIT ABOVE LAKE CORBARA

Distance/time: 13km; 4h
Grade: moderate, with an overall descent/ascent of 350m (the ascent is on the *return* route); few waymarks
Equipment: as pages 46-47
Refreshments: none
How to get there: 🚗 to Titignano (Car tour 2 at the 163km-point); no public transport
Note: swimming in the lake is not advisable; the water may be polluted.
Short walk: Titignano — Roccaccia

— Titignano: 6km; 1h45min; easy, 150m ascent. At the turn-off to the right below Titignano (10min) continue straight ahead on the wide descending track. This follows the ridge (good views) and passes an **old farm with a well.** Five minutes past here, turn right on a forest trail with red and white waymarks. This takes you in 10 minutes to the **ruins of the Roccaccia Castle.** Retrace your steps back to Titignano.

Between Todi and Orvieto the River Tiber winds its way for three kilometres through the steep wooded slopes of the Gola del Forello, before flowing into the Lago di Corbara. This artificial lake was created in 1962, when nearly all the roads around this part of the river were flooded. To the north of the lake there is an extensive harmonious landscape of rolling hills with vineyards, cornfields, olive groves, orchards and little woods, dotted with old farms and hamlets — like medieval Titignano, high above the lake. This walk, which leads from Titignano down to a cypress wood on the lake shore, offers fine views to the Gola del Forello and the calm waters of Lake Corbara.

Start the walk at the little **piazza in Titignano,** which you leave by going down some steps towards the lake. Then walk 50m to the left, to follow a wide descending track lined by cypresses. Ten minutes downhill, branch off right on another track, which passes an **old farmhouse** (**5min**). At this point, ignore the left turn to another farmstead. Beyond here the track narrows a bit, as it leads through broom and fig trees with views down to the lake. You pass two more old **farmhouses** (**25min**) and, 50m further on, come to a junction. Go left through a gate and skirt to the left of a vineyard for 100m, then cross the vineyard to the right.

Descending on the main trail, you pass another vineyard, this time on the left. You come onto a **grassy ridge,** with a farm track lined with olive trees. This is a good spot for a break, with views to Lake Corbara and back to the houses of Titignano,

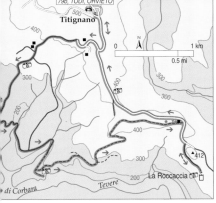

small paths lead 250m down to the steep and rocky shoreline of the Tiber, which at this point flows into Lake Corbara. The landscape, with its austere pine forests above the fjord-like lake, is more reminiscent of Nordic than Mediterranean climes. You can hear the traffic on the opposite shore.

Some 50m east of the white gravel shoulder with cypresses, take a small but clearly-seen path into the woods. You gain height in the shade of small deciduous trees. On coming to a T-junction (**2h05min**), go right; soon Lake Corbara comes into view. Ignore a turn-off to the right waymarked in blue (**2h25min**) and, still climbing, follow the path as it veers north, then northwest. Eventually reaching a clearing (**2h35min**), turn right and continue on a widening trail, now in an easterly direction, to a meadow. Pass to the right of a pond and follow the edge of the field to a track near an **old farm-house with a well** (**2h50min**).

From here it's worthwhile making a **diversion** to the ruin of La Roccaccia: follow the wide track toward the Tiber for almost five minutes, then turn right on a red-and white-waymarked trail. This takes you in 10 more minutes to the **ruin of Roccaccia Castle**, a pleasant place to take a break, with views down to the Gola del Forello (**3h05min**).

Retrace your steps from here to the old farmhouse with a well, where you keep to the main track. With views reaching over to Todi, climb steadily back to **Titignano** (**4h**).

Lake Corbara; below left: view of Todi

clinging to the hillside (**45min**). Walk along the ridge towards the Tiber River, crossing another vineyard. When it ends (before a stone trough), turn left, to meet a wide track some 100m further on (**55min**). Follow this to the left. The track eventually curves right and crosses a stream bed. For a few minutes you walk alongside the stream; then, curving left, you climb a short way up the hillside on an overgrown grassy trail. At the end of the bend, where a cobbled, steeper section begins, branch off right (**1h25min**; faded yellow arrow waymark).

A bit stony at first, this trail contours the southern hillside and descends in a curve to the right. You cross another stream bed and head south through a little wood. Eventually the trail peters out on a **white gravel hillside**, where **cypresses** grow in abundance (**1h50min**). From here

Walk 4: FROM SANTA RESTITUTA TO MONTE CROCE DI SERRA

Distance/time: 9km; 3h	**Equipment:** as pages 46-47
Grade: fairly easy-moderate, with an overall ascent/descent of 400m; stony paths; only the final ascent (20min) to the summit of Monte Croce is clearly waymarked in red	**Refreshments:** bar in Santa Restituta; none en route
	How to get there: 🚌 to Santa Restituta (Car tour 2 at the 111km-point); no public transport

To the south of the Gola del Forello (the gorge of the river Tiber), a mostly-barren limestone ridge runs towards Amelia. Monte Croce di Serra (994m) is the highest point on this unknown little mountain range in the southwest corner of Umbria. This is our goal, and we start at the remote village of Santa Restituta. The summit route, initially in the shade of oaks, later climbs scrubby, stony slopes. At several points you enjoy panoramic views over the surrounding countryside: to the west you look into the Tiber Valley with the shining waters of Lake Alviano and, to the east, over the widespread hills of the Todi landscape, where old farmhouses and villages stand crowded together on the hillocks, rather like fortified castles.

Start the walk at the lower entrance to the little historic centre of **Santa Restituta**, built against the slopes of the mountain. From the road leading to the village, go left through an arch between the houses and climb the steps of the central lane (Via T. Baolucci). At the top end of the lane you again walk under an arch; 100m beyond it, climb a small road to a left-hand bend at a green iron cross. Turn right here, on a level track (**10min**).

Ignore the turning to the left 50m along. You will follow this main track for half an hour, contouring the eastern hillside in gentle undulations. Some five minutes from the green iron cross you pass a little **stone hut housing a spring**, on your left. To the east the Martani Mountains appear (see Walk 9). Beyond a thin holm-oak wood, the track veers west for a short time, goes past a house shaded by some chestnut trees (**30min**) and describes a bend to the right. You again head north, with views to the old village of Toscolano.

When the track starts descending more steeply (**40min**) turn left on a stony and grassy trail (red arrow waymark on a stone). This climbs for three minutes, then passes through a fence (close the gate behind you!). Some 30m past the gate, turn left and follow a faint path south up a grassy ridge with junipers and broom. Continue through a rough hedge to the edge of the woods, where a path begins slightly to the right (occasionally waymarked with a red cross). Climbing gently, this runs along the western hillside for five minutes, to a T-junction just below a **saddle** (**55min**) in the woods.

Turn slightly to the right, to continue on a rising trail in a westerly direction. The forest gradually thins out and reveals views to the northeast over the extensive hills around Todi. Walking alongside a wire fence, you meet the end of a track, but leave it almost immediately, to climb up left onto the **barren ridge** (**1h10min**). From this treeless limestone ridge you have a fine view westwards down into the Tiber Valley.

Follow the ridge to the right on an initially flat trail, which five minutes

56

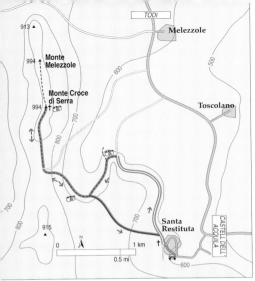

later begins gradually to ascend the southern slope of Monte Croce di Serra. Having climbed for around 100m, you meet a path with many red way-marks. Follow this through a dark little holm oak wood. At the end of the wood you reach the **summit of Monte Croce di Serra** (994m; **1h45min**), marked by a wooden cross. Here again you enjoy a panoramic view over the mountainous surroundings. Retrace your steps back down to the barren ridge and the **saddle** in the woods first encountered at the 55min-point in the outgoing walk (**2h30min**). Here you leave your outward route and continue on the trail straight ahead. This runs flat for 50m, then heads down to the right quite steeply — taking you quickly back to **Santa Restituta** (**3h**).

The ridge below Monte Croce di Serra

57

Walk 5: FROM ASSISI ACROSS MONTE SUBASIO TO SPELLO

Distance/time: 20km; just over 6h
Grade: fairly strenuous, because of the length and the long initial climb; ascent of some 800m, descent 950m; red and white waymarks (CAI50)
Equipment: as pages 46-47
Refreshments: kiosk near the Eremo delle Carceri
How to get there: 🚌 to Assisi (base for Car tour 3). 🚂 hourly trains from Spello to Assisi (S. Maria degli Angeli station), then frequent city buses to the centre. 🚌 from Spello (Viale Centrale Umbra, Bar Angolo) to Assisi (Piazza Matteotti) Mon-Sat

except school holidays
7.56, 14.08, 18.50
Walking map:
Carta dei Sentieri del Monte Subasio, Club Alpino Italiano, 1:20,000
Shorter walk:
Take a taxi for the 6km from Assisi to the Eremo delle Carceri and start there; 14km; 4h+; moderate, with an ascent of 450m

Many legends tell of Saint Francis of Assisi's love of nature and of how he withdrew into the forests of Monte Subasio for prayer and meditation. This long hike from Assisi to the medieval town of Spello follows in his footsteps. Past the Franciscan hermitage of Eremo delle Carceri with its ancient holm oaks, we rise up to the mountain pastures of the bleak summit ridge, from where we enjoy a superb panorama. This walk is at its best in early summer, when the wide grassy slopes are blanketed with flowers.

Start the walk at **Piazza Matteotti** at the uppermost eastern edge of **Assisi** (430m). Follow Via Santuario delle Carceri (🚶: Eremo delle Carceri), leaving Assisi via the Cappuccini Gate in three minutes. Immediately through the gate, turn left and climb alongside the city walls in the shade of some cypresses. On reaching the tower of **Rocca Minore** the trail veers right and becomes steeper. At a three-way-junction (**20min**), take the middle fork. There now follows a steep 30-minute ascent on a stony path, at the end of which you have a superb panorama down over Assisi and the Valle Umbra (**50min**). A flat path takes you from here to a road. Follow the road to the right, down to a junction 100m above the enclosure of the **Eremo delle Carceri** (730m; **1h15min**). The ongoing route to Monte Subasio turns left here (🚶: San Benedetto/

Bolzella). Follow the small surfaced road for five minutes, to a right-hand bend, where you branch off left on a trail (🚶: Vallonica). Continue through a thin wood, with a normally-dry stream on the left, steadily gaining height. Ignore a turn-off to the left. The path curves right, crosses a stream bed and eventually leads out of the wood onto the open grasslands of Monte Subasio. Climbing half-left, you come to the unmanned **Rifugio di Vallonica** (1059m; **2h**). Pass to the right of the building and continue to an animal watering place. Beyond here the path rises slightly in a hollow between barren hills, heading south. Veering a little to the left, you reach a wooden cross at grassy saddle with good views: **Sasso Piano** (1120m; **2h15min**). From here follow a clear path to the left. After a short flat section you come to another junction, where you

The map labels, reading across:

1100 800
1200
CA150
0 N 1 km
0.5 mi
Rifugio di Vallonica
900
1000
Eremo delle Carceri
CA150
500
▲ Monte Subasio
1290
Sasso Piano
Radio Subasio
SS75
Monte Civitella
1261
Mortaro Grande
Mortaiolo
CA152
1200
Fonte Bregno
1000
900
Fosso Renaro
914
Monte Pietrolungo
CA150
700
800
600
500
400
300
Spello
75

The Rocca Minore tower and the Castle of Assisi in morning mist

again turn left. Walk up through the treeless meadows of Monte Subasio to an unsurfaced road *(strada bianca)*, with the aerials of Radio Subasio behind it. Go right, alongside a fence, to a gap, then follow the road for several minutes, down to a hollow. From here continue left on a flat grassy trail which curves right and leads to two crater-like karst depressions: **Mortaro Grande** and **Mortaiolo** (1200m; **3h**).

The trail passes through these dolines and then heads a little to the right. You come to a drinking trough for animals; from here do *not* follow walking route 52 straight ahead, but turn 90° to the right and walk without any clear path back to the *strada bianca*. (For about 10 minutes orientation on this stretch is not always easy.) When you reach this unmade road, cross it *and* the fence behind it, then descend the open slope for 150m — to another, long watering place for cattle which can be seen ahead. Some stone troughs lie in a hollow 20m to the left. Again with no path, go 100m downhill alongside the hollow and watch for some wooden stakes on the left, which waymark the beginning of your ongoing path. With lovely views to the Monti Sibillini, this path descends diagonally until it meets a wider trail at the edge of the woods. Follow the trail 30m downhill, to the walled spring of **Fonte Bregno** (1000m; **3h30min**).

At the spring turn off sharp left. A pleasant path takes you down through oaks and hornbeams. The way curves right across a stream bed (**Fosso Renaro**) and, after a short

ascent reaches a track at the foot of **Monte Pietrolungo** (914m; **4h10min**). Follow this down to the right, crossing another track 10 minutes later. Descending through a pine wood you meet another track, which you follow downhill to the right for 10 more minutes. Enjoying panoramic views, you pass through typical dry Mediterranean vegetation, the air heavily scented with thyme, rosemary, broom and juniper. When the track curves left, take the trail branching off to the right. It descends to a motorable track in five minutes. Cross over and, 50m further on, join another, descending track. This panoramic route above olive plantations takes you down to **Spello**, which you enter by the old city gate (**Porta Montanara**; 290m; **5h45min**). It's another 10 minutes to the central Piazza Repubblica and around 15 minutes from here to the railway station — so a good **6h** in total.

Walk 6: the hermitage of Santa Maria Giacobbe

Walk 6: THE MENOTRE FALLS AND THE MONASTERY OF SASSOVIVO

See photograph opposite
Distance/time: 18km; 5h30min
Grade: moderate-strenuous because of the length and the overall ascent of about 700m
Equipment: as pages 46-47
Refreshments: bar with grocery shop at Uppello
How to get there: 🚌 from Foligno railway station to Belfiore, Mon-Sat at 7.42, 9, 10.05, 11.05, 12.35, 13.42; *no Sunday buses*. Return on 🚌 from Scandolaro to Foligno, Mon-Sat at 14.10, 16.50, 19.40; *no Sunday buses*. For info: www.umbria mobilita.it/orari/Servizi Urbani Foligno
Shorter walk: End the hike at Uppello; 14km; 4h; moderate. 🚌 to Foligno Mon-Sat at 14.20; *no buses on Sundays or school holidays*
Short circuit: 6km; 2h15min; easy. Coming down from Santa Maria Giacobbe to the junction first met five minutes outside Pale, turn right, descending a lovely trail, then track, through olive groves at the foot of rocky Sasso di Pale. After 15 minutes walk you're back at the earthen piazza at the end of Via Altolina.

This walk runs through the varied mountain landscape at the edge of the Valle Umbra east of Foligno. The route leads initially into the green valley of the Menotre stream, which drops steeply at the foot of the old village of Pale, forming three little waterfalls. High above, the hermitage of Santa Maria Giacobbe clings to the rocky cliffs of Sasso di Pale. From Pale we climb through typical macchia forest to the beautiful little medieval monastery of Sassovivo. The last section of the walk leads back into pleasant hilly countryside planted with olive trees, where we come upon the two tiny villages of Uppello and Scandolaro.

Start the walk at the eastern edge of **Belfiore**, at the last stop for buses coming from Foligno (turning area). Leaving the main road to Macerata, turn left on the smaller, slightly-rising Via Altolina (red/white/red waymarks), which enters the Menotre Valley. Follow this straight ahead for a good ten minutes, to a bridge on the right. From here you climb more steeply to the left for 100m, to where the tarmac finishes (**15min**). Two trails lead off here: take the one to the right (⌐: Sentiero natura); *the left fork is the return route for the Short circuit*.
The trail climbs past old olive trees, curves to the left in front of a stone house and leads up between walls at the left of a second house (set in a lovely panoramic position; **35min.**). A few steps behind this house, turn left on a path which leads after 30m to a **first little waterfall**.

The waymarked main route keeps on climbing as a sunken trail and passes an iron gate on the right; a few metres further on you have a good view down into a **rocky ravine** (keep away from the steep drop!). Some 50m further on, a **diversion** to the right past a picnic table, leads in three minutes to a shady place where the waters of Menotre flow out of a **dark cleft**.
Return to the main trail; a few minutes later it reaches a tile pipe sunk into the ground. From here make another **diversion** on the path to the left. Descend a short way alongside the edge of an olive grove, then turn right to the stream. Following it to the right you come to a pretty **second waterfall**, where you can cross the stream and look down to the first waterfall.
Retrace your steps and continue climbing the main trail. Past a **third**

waterfall you rises to **Pale** (475m; **1h10min** including the diversions). This old village, enclosed by a medieval defensive wall, was heavily damaged during the earthquake of 1997.

For the rewarding **diversion** to Santa Maria Giacobbe, turn left

beyond the village walls and go a short way down Via dell'Eremo. Then take a path straight ahead (at the right of a brick-built transformer tower). It contours along the steep rocky slopes of Sasso di Pale (958m) and comes to a Y-fork just five minutes from Pale. Go right here.

(The trail descending left here is the return route for the Short circuit.) The path zigzags up the steep hillside, in some places on steps with railings. It ends at the modest buildings of **Santa Maria Giacobbe** (**1h35min**) standing at the foot of vertical cliffs. During the 13th century a group of monks settled here, far away from the towns, and built the little church themselves, then had it painted with Biblical scenes.

Retrace your steps to **Pale** (**1h 50min**). Leave the village alongside the medieval walls, then continue past an old paper mill to the main Foligno/Colfiorito road. Opposite the junction, take a stony path, climbing into the scrubby woods (sparse red/white/red waymarks). At a T-junction five minutes later go right. The path climbs steeply for about another 20 minutes. Then, flattening out, it reaches a **saddle** and a woodland track (761m; **2h 40min**). Follow the wide track down to the right. At the following Y-fork, turn left (⌐: CAI66 Casale); Sassovivo Monastery comes into view below on the right. Then take a wide track downhill to the right, to a small road, which you follow 250m to the right. Past the ruin of the 11th-century **Cripta di Beato Alano** (with drinking-water spring) you arrive at the **Abbey of Sassovivo** with its beautiful cloister (**3h20min**).

Just before the abbey, 20m short of the right-hand bend in the road, your ongoing trail to Uppello turns off right (west). It climbs a few metres (no waymarks) to a viewpoint left towards the walls of Sassovivo, then flattens out. Follow a pleasant path along a wooded slope high above the valley. Some 15 minutes from Sassovivo, when you leave the woods, climb the hillside to the right, up to a little fenced-in concrete building. Beyond it, go straight ahead down a wide track. At a T-junction go left, descending more steeply, to a crossroads by a group of **houses with cypresses** and a shrine with a Madonna (**3h50min**). Continue left on a sunken track to **Uppello** (**4h**).

Leave the little piazza by the bar-grocery by heading left on the lane running underneath a house. Once out of Uppello you meet the small Foligno/Sassovivo Abbey road. Follow this 100m downhill, to where it bend right; go straight ahead here on a track. This descends through orchards to a dry stream bed and fades out. Walk left uphill alongside the stream bed through an olive grove to some fencing, where you cross the dry stream bed to the right. Then go right to a small road 50m away (**4h15min**).

Continue up the wide stony track opposite (⌐: Scandolaro 4km; red/white waymarks). A 10-minute climb takes you to a Y-fork in front of an olive grove: go left and, at the following junction 30m further on, take the track to the right. Now ascending slightly, you skirt to the left of the olive grove. Keep to the waymarked main track for some 45 minutes, contouring the hillside above the Valle Umbra with panoramic views. Eventually the track veers east towards the mountains and **Rocca Deli**, a small medieval castle, comes into view on a hillock to the right (**5h15min**). Nowadays it's an *agriturismo*.

Where the main track bends right (200m short of the castle), carry on straight ahead on a descending trail. At the junction 100m further on, turn right and follow the old mule trail through a broom-drenched valley, down to the village of **Scandolaro**. The central lane of this tiny, quiet village leads to the church square (**5h30min**), from where the buses leave for Foligno.

Walk 7: ACROSS THE OLIVE GROVES OF TREVI

Photographs on page 2 and 6
Distance/time: 17km; 5h10min
Grade: moderate, with an ascent of 580m; orientation is not always easy
Equipment: as pages 46-47; good shoes are sufficient
How to get there: 🚌 to Fonti del Clitunno (Car tour 3 at 100km); start the walk at the bar/café Le Ninfe by the main road. 🚌 from **Borgo Trevi** to Fonti del Clitunno: from the Via Cannaiola bus stop, Mon-Sat at 07.28, 13.46, 14.02 (*not during school holidays;* change at Pissignano); from the Colosseum bus stop, Mon-Sat at 15.08 (*but not Sat from mid-Jun to mid-Sep*), Mon-Fri at 17.16, 19.16. 🚌 from **Spoleto** (Ponte Sanguinario bus stop) to Fonti del Clitunno: Mon-Sat at 07.00, 10.55. Return by 🚌 from Trevi, daily at 15.52, 20.37; Mon-Sat at 15.20, 16.48, 19.37; Mon-Fri at 14.42, 17.11. Bus info: www.umbriamobilita.it/orari/Servizi Extaurbani Spoleto/line 423. Train info: www.trenitalia.com.

Shorter walk — circuit from Trevi: 10km; 3h; easy, with 300m ascent/ descent. From the large Piazza Garibaldi outside the old centre take the road to the right (⌐: Spoleto). Past the Carabinieri office take Via Orto degli Spiriti to the by-pass road. At the start of the next right-hand bend, turn left on the **smaller road up towards the cemetery**, but after 100m turn right on a track past an old house (private, keep out) and then the cemetery enclosure. Shortly after, ignore the main track leading up left to a farmhouse, but follow the smaller farm track straight ahead, climbing slightly through an olive grove. Having passed some big oaks, turn left with the main trail, rising steeply through olive trees, with a lovely view back towards Trevi. When the trail veers right and ends (**40min**), go straight ahead up a grassy path to the left of an old wall overgrown with brambles. After 10 more minutes of ascent follow the start of a farm track to the right for 200m. At a T-junction, turn left along a track on a ridge. Follow this uphill for 10 minutes, towards the hamlet of Costa San Paolo. 50m below a gate to a house, at a little pond on the right, take a chained-off trail to the right (**1h10min**). Descend steadily southwards through a thin oak wood. You pass a fountain on the left and 10 minutes later meet a major track. Turn left: in 10 minutes you reach the church of **Sant'Arcangelo** (**1h45min**), situated in a lovely panoramic position.

From here head down steps to the right of Sant'Arcangelo (red/white waymarks), to a path which descends steeply through an olive grove. On meeting a wider trail, follow it to the left, down to a small road, where you turn right. After 250m, beyond a **group of houses**, this becomes unsurfaced. 350m further on, turn right on a smaller track. Rounding a bend in the hillside you catch a fine glimpse of Trevi. Follow the flat trail north into a valley, where you come to a track (**2h15min**). Go up 10m to the right, then turn left on a red- and white-waymarked path. Pick up the main walk at the 3h45min-point, to return to **Trevi** (**3h**).

The small medieval town of Trevi, this walk's destination, stands with old walls, towers and gates on a hillock above the plains, an extremely attractive picture. Up here on the high slopes all is still idyllic. This walk rises and falls through a harmonious landscape of olive groves, passing two well preserved medieval castle villages — Campello Alto and Castello Pissignano, as well as the beautifully-sited church of Sant'Arcangelo.

From the **Bar-Café Le Ninfe** by the **Clitunno springs** (230m) walk 100m south on small Viale Silva e Lucia, parallel to the main road; then, opposite an oratory, take an earthen track uphill. It passes to the right of two houses, narrows to a grassy trail and climbs along the edge of a corn field to a group of houses (**10min**). Turn right on Via Virgilio. After 40m go left on Via Santa Rita, past the junction of Via San Francesco. Keep straight ahead on Via Santa Rita for 150m, to another group of houses. Branch off left here on smaller Via San Benedetto. Some 100m further on, in front of a wall, swing 10m left, to pick up an earthen trail shaded by tall pines. This winds between old walls to a small road which you follow uphill to the church of **Santa Maria** (308m; **25min**).

Climb some steps to the left of the door. Follow a track to the left, alongside an old wall, to the gate of a large villa (No 25). Take the gravel road ascending along the walls of this property towards Campello Alto, towering on the hilltop above. At the end of the enclosure fork left on a small track through bushes. At the left-hand bend three minutes later fork right on a shady path, after

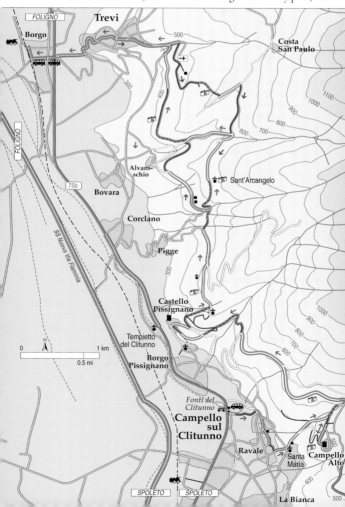

10 minutes descending to a **ditch** (**45min**). But just *before* the ditch take a faint farm track to the right: after 50m this narrows to a grassy path and rises beside an olive grove to a small road. Walk straight on, pass a large pink building with a church tower, and turn right above it to enter the tiny castle-like medieval village of **Campello Alto** (490m; **1h**) via an archway.

Return to the 45min-point and continue uphill, crossing the ditch. The path widens to a track and joins a small tarmac road (**1h20min**). It climbs west, with a nice view towards Campello Alto. At a sharp right-hand bend continue straight ahead on a wide track (⌐: Via di San Francesco; blue/yellow waymarks) until you come to a sharp left-hand bend (**1h55min**). Take the trail straight ahead here, into the olive groves. When it ends after 200m, by a lone oak tree, turn left down a steep blue/yellow waymarked path. Then the path contours through olive trees and pines towards the Valle Umbra, becoming a little stony. You descend to a wider trail where waymarked Via di San Francesco goes off right, but you continue straight ahead downhill. Cross a track and descend to the second fortified village, **Castello Pissignano** (325m, **2h20min**). Turn right about 30m before the entrance gate to the village, take some steps up to a track, and climb steeply away from the fortifications (red/white waymarks, Route 203). Five minutes up you meet another track. Follow it left for 200m, to a sharp right-hand bend, where you go straight ahead on a small path parallel with a telephone line. This climbs for 10 minutes through dense shrubs to a large walled **nunnery**. Turn left (yellow/blue waymarks of Via di San Francesco) and follow the wall 100m to the nunnery access track (525m; **2h45min**). Continue to the left on the track,

contouring the slopes with far-reaching views down to the plain. Pass a chapel on the left and come to a larger track (**3h05min**), which you descend for 10 minutes. When it becomes surfaced, turn right on a trail into an olive grove (red and white waymarks). This passes to the right of a villa and climbs a little way, to a concrete track. Climb this track, which veers left and becomes unsurfaced. Some 50m beyond a restored stone house you leave the Via di San Francesco, turning sharp right on a steeply-climbing trail *(no waymarks)*. This narrows to a path which rises to the church of **Sant' Arcangelo**, with a lovely view over the Valle Umbra (550m; **3h35min**). From here follow the wide track heading north. Ten minutes along, this bends left and descends more steeply through a stand of trees. Just under 20 minutes from Sant'Arcangelo, turn right on a level, red- and white-waymarked path (**3h55min**) running along the south side of the hill; you immediately pass an **old stone house**. *(The Shorter walk from Trevi joins here.)* You now walk on the traces of a **Roman aqueduct**, contouring to an old restored stone house, where the path widens to a track. Continue in a northerly direction through olive groves, with lovely views towards Trevi. Meet a road and keep ahead, then fork left at a junction, into the old centre of **Trevi** (425m; **4h45min**).

For the railway station/bus stop in Borgo Trevi, you have to descend via a maze of lanes. Eventually veering left, leave the *centro storico* and follow a secondary road to the right, into **Borgo Trevi**. Cross the main Foligno/Spoleto road and continue on Via Cannaiola, passing the Colusseum bus stop after 40m and crossing Via Faustana/Via Sant'Egidio. On the left 40m after the crossroads is the Cannaiola bus stop. Now it's just three minutes to the **railway station** (**5h10min**).

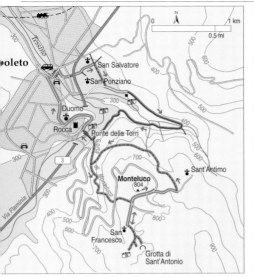

Distance/time:
10km; 3h20min
Grade: easy-moderate, with an overall ascent/descent of around 450m
Equipment: as pages 46-47
Refreshments: bar, restaurant at Monteluco
How to get there: the walk starts in the centre of Spoleto (base for Car tours 4 and 5)
Note: on weekends the Monteluco area can be very crowded.

Spoleto is one of the few rare towns — even in Italy — where you can see find unspoilt nature virtually on the doorstep of the historical centre. At the back of the papal castle, Rocca Albornoz, the famous medieval Ponte delle Torri leaps over the deep valley of the Tessino stream, and beyond rise the steep wooded slopes of the 'Holy Mountain of Monteluco'.

This circuit is not very long, but the ascents lift the grade beyond easy. We follow the cobbled 'Corta di Monteluco' pilgrims' trail uphill, sheltered by ancient holm oaks, to a modest monastery founded by Saint Francis. The sacred woods of Monteluco have been protected since 241BC under an ancient law, the 'Lex Spoletina', inscribed on a stone tablet. The medieval hermits and monks still obeyed this rule, which banned tree-felling. That's why this tall forest of holm oaks, the dominant wood throughout Italy since antiquity, is still so well preserved.

Start the walk on **Piazza della Vittoria** at the lower edge of **Spoleto**'s *centro storico*. Walk out of town across the Tessino stream on the large Ponte Garibaldi bridge, which is built over Roman walls. Over the bridge, turn right and then left, to follow Via C. Micheli. When this ends, go up some steps and take the path beneath the expressway. Then climb past a turning right towards medieval San Ponziano to

the early medieval church of **San Salvatore**, built by reusing columns from a Roman temple (**10min**). Opposite San Salvatore follow a short path 100m uphill through a meadow with some olive trees towards Spoleto Castle. At the top of the path you meet a concrete track, which you climb to the left. Walk steeply uphill for five minutes, to a house on the right, where the track becomes unsurfaced and

67

delle Torri you cross the surfaced road to Monteluco. Some 15 minutes later you are walking alongside the walls of the little **Santuario di San Francesco**. The monastery entrance is reached beyond the Albergo Ferretti (**1h45min**).

A **diversion** of 20 minutes now takes you to some good viewpoints: leaving the monastery, veer a little to the right, go through a gate and into a stand of holm oaks. At the three-way junction 100m further on, the fork furthest to the left leads to the **Grotta di Sant'Antonio**, a cave where, according to legend, Saint Anthony used to meditate. The path furthest to the right descends to **two balcony viewpoints**; from the lower one the towers of Spoleto are visible.

Retrace your steps to the **Albergo Ferretti** (**2h05min**), then go straight ahead past the Albergo Paradiso to the Spoleto/Monteluco road. Follow it a short way down to the left, then turn right downhill on a smaller road. Five minutes later this approaches the one-time hermitage of **Sant'Antimo**. At the edge of the large meadow extending towards the building, take a clear path off left, skirting the wood. At the lower end of the grassy slope, the path veers left into the forest. Sheltered by holm oaks, you regain the Corta di Monteluco (**2h50min**), which you follow back down to **Ponte delle Torri** (**3h05min**).

Walk across the bridge, high above the Tessino Gorge, and round the castle hill, to reach Piazza Campello. From here a series of pedestrian lanes (Via Saffi/Via Fontesecca/ Piazza Planciani/Via Nervio/Via Salaria Vecchia/Via dei Porta Fuga/Corso Garibaldi) lead down past the **cathedral square** and back to the starting point, **Piazza della Vittoria** in **Spoleto** (**3h20min**).

flattens out. With a lovely view to Spoleto Castle and the Ponte delle Torri spanning the gorge, continue straight ahead in an easterly direction. Past another old house, continue into a valley. At the end of the valley, cross a ditch to the right on a little bridge, then turn right again on a level, red- and white-waymarked trail. With more splendid views to the *rocca,* this trail contours the hillside above the deep gorge-like valley of the Tessino, and takes you to the **Ponte delle Torri** (**40min**).

Above the near end of the bridge, by the ruined Fortezza dei Mulini, take a trail rising to the left (red and white waymarks, Sentiero 1). You are now on the old pilgrims' route, the **Corta di Monteluco**, quickly gaining height as you wind uphill in the shade of the holm oaks. The route is lined by hermits' deserted chapels and shrines. After around 40 minutes walking from the Ponte

Walk 9: FROM CESI ACROSS MONTE TORRE MAGGIORE TO THE RUINS OF CARSULAE

Distance/time: 14km; 4h45min to Carsulae (to San Gemini station add 2.5km; 35min)
Grade: fairly strenuous, with an overall ascent of 750 m
Equipment: as pages 46-47; take sufficient drinking water
Refreshments: bars at the entrance to Carsulae and in Fonte Sangemini
How to get there: 🚗 to Cesi (Car tour 4 at the 32km-point). 🚌 to Cesi (Mon-Sat 8 buses, Sun 3). Return from Carsulae to Cesi/Terni by 🚌 Mon-Sat at 15.09, 18.19. Info: www.umbriamobilita.it/orari/ Servizi Extraurbani/Terni/line E 616. Return from San Gemini station by 🚆 daily at 18.41; Mon-Sat at 15.47, 20.57; Mon-Fri (not Jul/Aug) at 14.59, 17.08, 19.46; Sun at 15.54, 20.31. Info: www.umbria mobilita.it/Servizi Ferroviari.
Variation — Circuit from Cesi: 13km; 4h40min; grade as main walk. Follow the main walk to

Monte Torre Maggiore, then descend to the track below and turn left. After 10 minutes you return to the **Cisterne Nuove**, from where you retrace your steps down to **Sant'Erasmo (3h40min)**. Here go left alongside the polygonal terrace wall, then turn left on a trail down through woods. The trail veers right, down through a stream bed, and is very stony for a short time. After eventually passing two stone huts you meet a track. Head down right, past a villa with a cypress, to the Terni/Cesi road and turn right; you reach Cesi five minutes later. Climb up right, through a gate, into the old centre (bar, panorama terrace on Piazza Umberto I).
Short walk — Circuit from Sant' Erasmo: 7km; 2h30min; easy-moderate, with 450m ascent/ descent. Pick up the main walk at the 1h10min-point, then follow the circuit above from Torre Maggiore.

The foundations of a temple more than 2500 years old were discovered on Monte Torre Maggiore (1120m) in the Monti Martani north of Terni. Like nearly all ancient sanctuaries, it was built in an area of great scenic beauty. From this holy mountain of pre-Roman Umbria you enjoy a wide panorama to the Apennines and mountains of Latium (Lazio), with Monte Terminillo (2284m) as the highest point. You also come upon ancient and medieval relics up here. Carsulae, today a picturesque ruin, was once an important Roman town on the Via Flaminia. Simple Romanesque architecture defines the Franciscan hermitage of L'Eremito and the little church of Sant'Erasmo, the latter built over the polygonal walls of another early Umbrian temple.

Start the walk in **Cesi** (437m) at the pharmacy (farmacia) on the main road below the centro storico. Take Via Arnolfo opposite the farmacy, climbing into the old town. At the grocery, 100m further on, turn left on little Via Santa Maria. Past the church, you ascend to Piazza Cesi, from where you go left through a gate, out of town. Beyond the gate walk up the small road towards Sant'Erasmo for three

minutes, to a left-hand bend with a large concrete retaining wall on the right. Continue past it, to where a red- and white-waymarked path starts on the right.
This climbs steeply east through a valley with limestone cliffs towering above. After 20 minutes of strenuous ascent the path turns left and the gradient eases. The path runs along a terraced slope, with a ditch on the left. After walking

Sant'Erasmo

parallel with the stream bed for 100m, you come to a junction in the woods. Turn right on a path with *yellow* waymarks; it climbs steeply for 50m and then curves right in a more southerly direction. The small path leads through the forest to the ruins of a **medieval castle** (45min). Go the left, alongside the walls, and steeply uphill to the upper tower. To the left of it a path with old, faded red and yellow waymarks takes you back into the woods. After 10 more minutes of ascent through the forest you'll see a wall with large polygonal blocks above you; they form a flat terrace. They are the foundations of an Umbrian temple dating from the 5th century BC, over which the small church of **Sant'Erasmo** was erected in medieval times (787m; **1h10min**).

From here follow the small road coming from Cesi 300m uphill, to where it bends slightly left. Here take the upper, red- and white-waymarked, stony trail to the right, past a no entry sign (for vehicles). Ascend through a thin forest to a clearing, which is crossed to the left. Further on, the trail veers slightly to the right and leads across a meadow on a flat ridge, to the foot of Monte Torre Maggiore. Here you can see a track coming up from Sant'Erasmo over to the left (**1h50min**). Ignore this; instead take a trail to the right which descends a short way. You pass the picnic area and concrete watering troughs of **Cisterne Nuove** on the left, then follow a flat trail along wooded slopes. At a Y-fork five minutes later, go left (red waymarks). The lovely path winds its way through a holm oak forest, contouring along the southern slopes of Monte Torre Maggiore. After around 20 minutes it leaves the woods and reaches a flat open ridge with a **round pond** (**2h15min**).

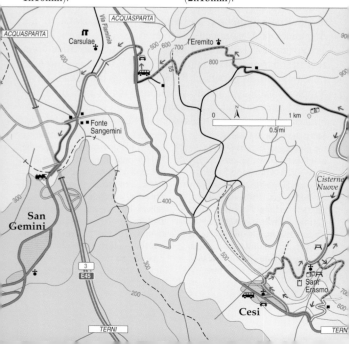

Behind the pond turn left (north) on a reddish, stony path. This ascends the left side of the ridge dropping down from Monte Torre Maggiore and offering fine views towards Sant'Erasmo and the bleak mountains above the Valnerina. Beyond a hollow with a pile of stones (**2h30min**) the now-fainter trail becomes steeper. Keeping a little to the right of a white rocky outcrop, you come to the edge of a stand of pines. From here it's only a three-minute walk to the left, to the flat summit of **Monte Torre Maggiore** (1122m; **2h50min**) with its fenced-in but freely accessible excavations.

From the archeological site take a trail heading northwest down the treeless slopes. Beyond a fence you meet the main track coming up from Sant'Erasmo, which you follow 200m to the right. *(Turn left here for both Circuit variations.)* When you see two wooden posts, fork left onto the high grassy plain (**3h05min**). Continue to the left of a wooden enclosure, crossing the wide bare ridge. Walk through a hollow with a high tension line, climb a short way back up, and come to a **little house with a tiled roof** (**3h30min**). Turn left in front of the house, to walk downhill alongside a fence, through a meagre forest. At the lower end of the fenced-in area, veer right, to meet a track by a gate on the right (**3h40min**). Follow the track down to the left for 50m, then fork right on a scrubby path with red and white waymarks. This quickly takes you to a clearing, where you veer a little to the left and take a path descending through a shady forest. The path meets a track near the hermitage of l'Eremito (**3h55min**).

Turn left in front of the monastery enclosure on an old mule trail running alongside a moss-covered drystone wall (red and white waymarks). After a section through boulders, the lovely path descends beneath distorted old holm oaks. After around 15 minutes from l'Eremito the main path curves sharply to the right (yellow/red waymarks; Sentiero 55), still running through woods. Two clearings afford nice outlook points. When you come to a junction, go left. The countryside opens out, and you descend through fields to a track coming from a villa, which you follow to the Cesi/Acquasparta road (**4h35min**).

The bus to Cesi stops here (blue sign). But we follow the road a short way to the right, to a car park. From here an underpass beneath the road leads to the entrance to **Carsulae** (**4h45min**). Only a few ruins are left from the Roman town — for example a quite long and well-preserved section of the cobbled Via Flaminia. The remote setting of the excavations, on an extensive grassy terrace sheltered by large trees, is very appealing.

On to San Gemini station: From the entrance to Carsulae follow the pale dirt road south for 200m, to a small surfaced road with little traffic. This takes you down to the group of houses by the mineral spring of **Fonte Sangemini** (**5h**). Cross the main road, follow the side road SP41 200m towards Montecastrilli. At a barrier turn sharp left on a trail under oaks. After five minutes it passes a first ruin and veers a little to the left at a second one, running downhill across a meadow. At the bottom keep to the left of some houses and cross the railway line on a road bridge to small **San Gemini station** (**5h20min**).

Walk 10: FROM FERENTILLO TO SAN PIETRO IN VALLE

Distance/time: 14km; 4h45min
Grade: moderate, with an overall ascent/descent of 680 m
Equipment: as pages 46-47
Refreshments: restaurant at the monastery of San Pietro; bar, pizzeria in Macenano

How to get there: 🚗 to Ferentillo (Car tour 4 at the 107km-point); 🚌 fairly frequent daily buses Terni/Ferentillo/Scheggino
Walking map: Carta dei Sentieri del Comprensorio Spoletino 1:50,000 (CAI), but lacking in detail

This walk leads into the varied mountain landscape around Ferentillo, with its limestone cliffs, dark green Mediterranean woods and stony high meadows. In the old villages many ruins testify to the past century's migration to the cities. After a long initial climb past deserted Gabbio and the still-inhabited village of Lorino, we descend to the monastery of San Pietro in Valle. This medieval building, beautifully-sited amid cypresses and olive trees on a terraced slope above the Valnerina, is a jewel of Romanesque architecture. The return follows the pleasant Nera Valley, with a detour to the ruined hamlet of Umbriano.

Starting point is the Piazza Garibaldi in the centre of **Ferentillo-Materello** (250m). From here go up the steps of Via della Rocca. At the first right-hand bend walk straight ahead on a slightly-overgrown path, passing a shed to the right (red/white/red waymarks). When you come to a track, walk a few paces to the left, then turn right. The wide track ascends northwest through olive groves. Beyond a sharp right-hand bend, turn left (⌐: Nicciano Sentiero 0.45h; red/white/red waymarks). This old old cobbled trail rises to the picturesque hamlet of **Gabbio**, completely abandoned by its former inhabitants (340m; **35min**).

Continue on the path to the right of the little church, contouring the western hillside. The path becomes flat and offers far-reaching views to the west. At the junction a good 15 minutes outside Gabbio, ignore the red waymarks pointing to the left; continue straight ahead. This route follows the old mule trail to Lorino, soon zig-zagging steeply uphill. You pass a covered ruin on the right. At the following junction go left, keeping to the old trail with stone steps. Having crossed a patch of

wood, you skirt above an overgrown olive grove and go through a stretch of trail hemmed in by dense gorse. Beyond there, take the trail furthest to the right, alongside a fence. This soon meets the wide track to Lorino (**1h25min**). Climb this track for some 10 minutes, to a sharp bend to the right, then, 50m past the bend, take a path to the left, up to the little church of **Lorino** (700m; **1h40min**). Some people still live here all year round.

Leave Lorino on the main track to the north. This ascends a little towards the impressive bulk of isolated Monte Solenne, then flattens out and runs alongside a pine forest. After around 30 minutes from Lorino you reach a saddle, where the track ends near a **ruin** at the foot of the barren stony slopes of Monte Solenne.

The ongoing route to San Pietro branches off right a short way before the saddle. The trail passes through an iron barrier (**2h10min**), then drops, initially running between fences and through pine forest. For a moment the monastery of San Pietro comes into sight. Follow this main route for quite a while, descending steeply past a farm building. Watch

72

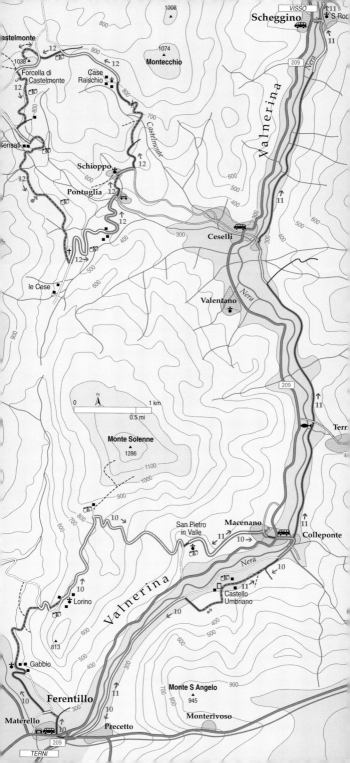

Ferentillo (above) and saddle at the foot of Monte Solenne (left)

for a trail with a wooden railing on the left, which takes you in two minutes to **San Pietro Monastery (3h)**.

From here follow the wide access track lined by cypresses. You can see the ruins of the Castello Umbriano on the slopes on the far side of the valley. The track becomes surfaced and leads to **Macenano (3h20min)**. At the village fountain, turn right between the houses onto Via di Macenano. Leave the hamlet by taking stone steps on the left. Where these curve to the right, go straight ahead on a path. You come to another lane with steps, which takes you down to the main Valnerina road. Cross it and walk down Via di Colle Ponte, over the river Nera and to the village of **Colleponte (3h30min)**.

Beyond the bridge follow the road a

74

short way to the right. At the following junction, turn right across a small water channel. Some 50m after the tarmac ends, go left towards Umbriano. (The track to the right would lead more directly back to Ferentillo.) At the following bend to the left, fork straight ahead on a smaller track. At the following Y-fork, take the path to the right, contouring the western hillside. In the shade of trees, you come to the ruins of **Castello Umbriano (4h)**, which was finally deserted around 1900. Contour the hillside to the left through the ruins and continue on a path, circling down to the right (orange waymarks). Beyond a spring the path widens out and descends to the track in the bottom of the valley **(4h20min)**. In the shade of high-rising mountains you follow this pleasant route downstream, to **Ferentillo-Precetto**. Cross the bridge over the river Nera and, on the far side, take a stepped trail up to Piazza Garibaldi in **Ferentillo-Materello (4h45min)**.

Walk 11: THROUGH THE VALNERINA FROM SCHEGGINO TO PIEDIPATERNO

Distance/time: 11.5km; 3h30min
Grade: easy, with 230m of ascent
Equipment: as pages 46-47; good shoes are sufficient
Refreshments: bar below Sant' Anatolia, on the main road by the turn-off to Gavelli
How to get there: 🚌 from Piedipaterno to Scheggino Mon-Sat at 8.09, 16.10, 17.16 (Contram Macerata-Terni line); Mon-Fri at 14.32 *(not in school holidays)*; Sun, Nov-Feb at 16.10, Mar-Oct at 17.16; Info: www.umbria mobilita.it/orari/ Servizi Extraurbani Spoleto/lines E 432-433 and www.contram.it.

Shorter walk: 9km; 2h50min; easy. 🚌 from Piedipaterno to Sant' Anatolia as above and also at 9.33 (Sun), 12.09 (Mon-Sat), 14.38 (daily), 16.33 (Mon-Sat), 18.53 (daily); line E 401 Norcia-Spoleto. From the Bar Tre Valli on the main road follow the small road towards Gavelli for 150m. Beyond the bridge over the Nera turn left on the red/ white waymarked track towards Castel San Felice, which passes to the left of an old fountain. Pick up the main walk at the 45min-point.
Longer walk: Ferentillo to Borgo Cerreto (2 days): see page 77.

Walking is undoubtedly the best way to enjoy the idyllic scenery of the Valnerina, the steeply-sloping valley of the river Nera, with its old villages and meadows thick with wild flowers. To see the loveliest stretch — from Ferentillo in the south, where the valley narrows almost to a gorge, to Borgo Cerreto in the north, beyond which the old trail has disappeared beneath a road — takes two days of easy walking (see page 77). The day walk described here covers the middle stretch, from Scheggino to Piedipaterno, and runs a little away above the valley. We walk through oak forests and along meadows full of gorse, with lovely views over the valley. En route is the remote medieval village of Vallo di Nera, perched on a hill; anywhere but in Italy, this would certainly be a well-known tourist sight!

Starting point is the river bridge in the centre of **Scheggino**. Head north on the small road along the eastern bank, parallel with the river. You pass to the left of the San Rocco chapel. At a right-hand bend after five minutes (beyond house No 22), continue straight ahead on a track. After five more minutes the track narrows and climbs a little to the right as a pleasant forest trail above the river bank. You meet another track and follow it straight ahead to the new settlement at the edge of **Sant'Anatolia di Narco (35min)**. Continue a short way on the road to the right of the houses. When the road curves left, go straight ahead, across the road to Gavelli, into little **Piazza Corrado** by the old city walls

(Mura Urbiche) and the church of Santa Maria delle Grazie (14-16C, with frescoes by the Master of Eggi from around 1450).

The ongoing route to Castel San Felice, already visible to the north, descends the small road to the right of the Mura Urbiche. You cross a wider road, then take a trail down right, crossing the same road once more. Then follow a track to the left of an **old fountain** which leads into the valley (**45min**; ⏱: S. Maria di Narco; red and white waymarks; Sentiero 13). *(The Shorter walk joins here.)* Always keeping to the flat main track, you reach the medieval river bridge below the simple Romanesque church of **Castel San Felice (1h05min)**.

You now leave the river valley and take the track just in front of the bridge, going uphill to the right *(no waymarks)*. At the junction a good five minutes later, turn right on a stony trail, climbing steeply. At a first distinct bend to the right, ignore a grassy trail straight ahead. Instead, climb another 100m on the main trail, to a second sharp right-hand bend, where you *do* take the smaller trail straight ahead

(**1h25min**). Constantly ascending, this trail passes below a high tension line and narrows to a path (overgrown in places) which veers a little to the east. After a clear section through woods the path reaches a stream near a **watering place for cattle** and a fence (**1h55min**). Take the trail leading off left here, which soon contours the hillside to the right, offering a lovely view over the Valnerina and towards the old

village of Vallo di Nera. The trail, now virtually level, runs in an easterly direction until passing a few metres above an old stone shed on the left. Turn left just past here, dropping steeply at first. The trail then flattens out and circles to the left above the valley. Past a spring (with trough) you join a wide track coming up from the left, which you follow for a few paces. Then turn left on an old mule trail. Past the little 15th-century church of **Immagine delle Force**, decorated with frescoes, you rise up to the medieval walls of **Vallo di Nera** (**2h45min**). Walk down between the old houses to the Palazzo Comunale. Beyond it, the old church of Santa Maria has interesting frescoes (14th/15th century).

From the Palazzo Comunale go down the steps between two car parks. Then take the sunken old trail, descending between drystone walls. (If it's too overgrown, go a few paces to the right and walk down the grassy slopes below the Hotel Cacio, parallel with the trail.) The trail passes an old fountain, becomes wider and veers a little to the right downhill. After a distinct left-hand bend (around 10 minutes from Vallo di Nera), take a trail branching off straight ahead towards the river. Then, 100m further on, turn right on another trail (a bit overgrown in places). After a short climb, this runs along a steep bank above the Nera. You come to a track and follow it for a few minutes, to the river bridge below **Piedipaterno** (**3h30min**). Buses stop on the far side, in front of the Bar Valnerina (where they sell bus tickets).

Variation — two-day walk from Ferentillo to Borgo Cerreto via Scheggino: Walks 11 and 12 can easily be combined to make a two-day excursion. On the first day we walk from Ferentillo to Scheggino, on the second from there to Borgo

Cerreto. Easily-followed, pleasant tracks run along the river valley between Colleponte and Scheggino and between Piedipaterno and Borgo Cerreto. Scheggino is a good place to spend the night, in the hospitable hotel-restaurant Albergo del Ponte.

First day — from Ferentillo to Scheggino: 14km; 4h30min; easy, with 200m of ascent; bars in Mace-

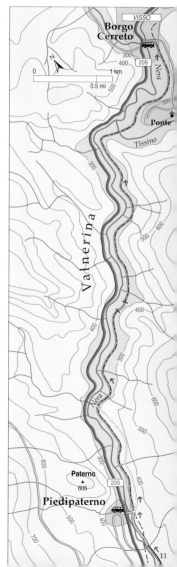

nano and Ceselli. Map on page 73. From Ferentillo to Colleponte we could take the route of Walk 10 through the mountains via Gabbio and Lorino, which is a good hour's walk longer than I propose and calls for an additional 400m of ascent. So it is easier to trace the last section of Walk 10 in reverse, as follows. From the bridge over the Nera near Ferentillo-Precetto follow the track upstream along the eastern bank of the river. After around 30 minutes take a narrow track off right (orange waymarks). This climbs steeply at first and circles uphill to the left. Once past a spring, the track narrows to a path and brings you to the ruined village of **Castello Umbriano** (**55min**), perched on the rocky edge of the hillside. On the slopes on the opposite side of the valley the monastery of San Pietro is visible. The path leads through the castle ruins and then veers right and descends to a track. Keeping straight ahead, you come to a surfaced road and the river bridge at **Colleponte** (**1h15min**).

For the one hour's **diversion to San Pietro Monastery** cross the bridge and the main road, then go up steps

78

to **Macenano**. Past the fountain you meet a small road. Follow this left for 20 minutes (eventually as a wide earthen track lined by cypresses), to the monastery of **San Pietro in Valle**.

Then return to the bridge at **Colleponte** (**2h15min**). From here follow the pleasant track on the eastern bank of the Nera north upstream. Beyond a big trout farm you cross the secondary road to Terria (**2h40min**). Always keep to the main track near the river. At a Y-fork under a high tension line, go left. A little later the old villages San Valentino and Ceselli come into view on the opposite hillside. Eventually joining a surfaced road, you reach the first houses of **Ceselli** (**3h35min**; bar on the far side of the river bridge). Keep to the right of the river, following Via Dicontro. Just following the main track through the valley, without any noticeable ascents, walk on to **Scheggino** (**4h30min**).

Second day — from Scheggino to Borgo Cerreto: 17km; 5h30min; moderate, with 280m of ascent; bars in Sant'Anatolia and Piedipaterno. 🚌 from Borgo Cerreto to Ferentillo Mon-Sat at 8.00, 16.01, 17.06 (Contram Macerata-Terni line); Sun, Nov-Feb at 16.01, Mar-Oct at 17.06; Info: www.umbriamobilita. it/orari/Servizi Extraurbani Spoleto/ lines E 433 and www.contram.it. Maps on pages 76 and 77. Follow Walk 11 to **Piedipaterno**. Then take the track along the eastern bank of the river, through the narrowing valley, below high rocky slopes. You are following the traces of the old Spoleto/Norcia railway line, and you pass through some short tunnels. Below the hamlet of Ponte (**5h**) you cross the Tissino stream and reach a small road. Turn left here, and in 15 minutes you come into **Borgo Cerreto** (**5h30min**).

Walk 12: LONELY MOUNTAINS ABOVE THE VALNERINA

See map on page 73
Distance/time: 15km; 4h30min
Grade: quite strenuous, with 700m
of ascent/descent; orientation needs
care on the first stretch from
Pontuglia to Case Raischio

Equipment: as pages 46-47
Refreshments: none
How to get there: 🚗 to Pontuglia,
3km east of Ceselli (the 121km-
point in Car tour 4); 🚌 Terni/
Scheggino line buses stop at Ceselli

Between Spoleto at the southern edge of the Valle Umbra and
the Valnerina further to the east, a nameless mountain range
rises to more than 1000m. After a long period of emigration, the
few villages and hamlets in this area are sparsely populated, some
are deserted and in ruins. Dense mixed forests grow on the
mountain slopes, and the barren summit ridges are covered by
meadows and stony pastures. This walk follows old trails, with a
long initial climb onto Castelmonte, an isolated rocky outcrop
with a superb panoramic view. The return route is especially
pleasant, on an old mule trail high above the valley of Pontuglia.

Starting point is the old hamlet of
Pontuglia (365m), 3km to the west
of Ceselli in Valnerina. From
building No 6, the old mill on the
valley road, climb 20m to the houses
and turn right, passing behind a
pond. Then take the second arched
entrance to the left, a dark passage
underneath the old houses. Beyond
it you come to an old tower-like
building, where you turn left on a
grassy trail, climbing past the last
houses of Pontuglia to a surfaced
track. This bends sharp left some
50m further on (in front of an little
concrete water storage building).
Just 20m past here, fork right on the
old path to Schioppo. You climb
steadily north through a sparse
wood. Above you, a steep rock face
comes into view, with the few
houses of **Schioppo** at the end
(475m; **20min**). At the first
building, veer right down a lane,
after 50m passing the little medieval
church of San Nicola di Bari (with
some good frescoes; key in the
house next to the church).
Continue for 150m on the small
road leading to the hamlet. Past the
entrance to a newer house, turn left
on an ascending farm track, skirting
above the meadows of Schioppo. At
the foot of the mountain slope the

route veers right. At the end of the
trail (**40min**) turn a little to the left,
to follow a path running
approximately parallel to electricity
wires. Ignoring a turn-off to the left,
contour along the eroded hillside
and cross the dry bed of **Fosso del
Castelmonte**. Then climb left for 10
minutes, following a stony and
partly-overgrown small path alongside the stream bed. When you come
to a pylon you walk under the
electricity wires again, to follow a
grassy trail straight ahead. Veering a
little to the right, go uphill past
sloping meadows, to the remote
group of houses called **Case
Raischio** (785m; **1h05min**).
Take the track at the right of the tiny
chapel; this ascends within 25
minutes to a **saddle**, a good place
for a break, with some shady pines
and a panorama extending from
Monte Subasio near Assisi to Monte
Terminillo in Lazio. Fork left at the
saddle on an ascending forest trail.
In 10 minutes you rise to a wide
track (**1h40min**). Just before
continuing to the left, climb the
rocky hill of Castelmonte, ahead of
you in the east, by taking the red-
and white-waymarked path opposite. This contours the northwestern
slope to the top of **Castelmonte**

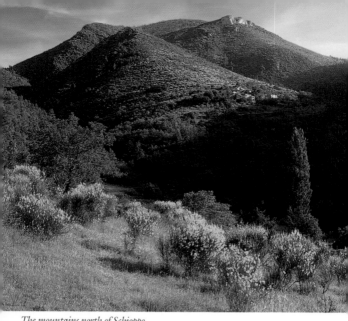

The mountains north of Schioppo

(1038m; **1h50min**), a pleasant viewpoint over the mountains of the Valnerina.

Return down to the main track and follow it south. Some 100m along, you pass the ruins of Casa Castelmonte and descend gently to a saddle, **Forcella di Castelmonte** (950m; **2h05min**), where you take a path to the left (►: Sensati sentiero 3; red and white waymarks). Go 100m downhill on a grassy path to the right of a flat gully, veering a little to the right, then drop more steeply 30m to the left, to join to a pretty path on the right. This runs along a terrace in the hillside, high above a rocky valley on the left, with a far-reaching views, then zigzags down more steeply to a restored house and a track. Follow the track to the right for 50m, to a T-junction. Turn left on a gently-descending track, in five minutes coming to the ruins of **Sensati** hamlet, completely overgrown with thorny bushes and wild roses full of rose-hips in the autumn (800m; **2h40min**).

At the end of the track to the hamlet, just in front of a ruin, turn sharp left on a path. After 50m you walk between two particularly large trees and the path veers down right, into a stream bed below Sensati. Keep to the right of this, watching out for occasional red and white waymarks. The path descends through a forest and leads right across a clearing (some 10 minutes from Sensati), then zigzags down, again in the shade of woods. After a stretch with superb views down to the Valnerina, you pass a rocky ravine with a little waterfall on the right. The easily-followed path leads past another good viewpoint and, half an hour from the little waterfall, you reach a track behind the **cemetery of le Cese** (**3h45min**).

Descend this wide track, with fine views over idyllic rural countryside. The track curves down to a **group of houses** (**4h05min**) and becomes a surfaced, although little-used road. Twenty minutes downhill, you're back in **Pontuglia** (**4h30min**).

Walk 13: IN THE MOUNTAINS ROUND GAVELLI

Distance/time: 11km; 3h45min
Grade: moderate; overall ascent/descent about 450m; almost no shade
Equipment: as pages 46-47
Refreshments: none en route
How to get there: 🚌 to Gavelli (a detour at the 206km-point on Car Tour 5); no public transport
Variation from Monte San Vito: 10km; 3h30min; moderate (overall ascent/descent of 680m). 🚌 to Monte San Vito (a detour at the 121km-point on Car Tour 4). In front of the first houses of **Monte San Vito** (930m) turn right on the track (⚑: Monte dell'Eremita 7km),

climbing east along the southern hillside. The Nera Valley, with the dramatic Ferentillo mountains opens up deep below. After 15 minutes the track descends a bit and bends right. Go left here on a path which zigzags northeast up the hillside, to a **watering place** with two long troughs. 150m further on (**1h**), pick up the main walk at its 2h15min-point. Follow the path along the southern slopes of Monte dell' Eremita to the **third gully** (1h30min), then turn left up to the summit ridge to complete the circuit

A walk of wide horizons, across a long, barren and windy ridge arched over by a high blue sky, where sometimes eagles soar. Large meadows, where only a few stands of gnarled small beech trees push against the wind, cover the flat summit of Monte dell'Eremita (1546m), but in early spring thousands of crocuses bloom up here. You look out east over uninhabited mountains, where wild cats, porcupines and even wolves feel at home.

Starting point is the little village of **Gavelli** (1150m). From the main road walk down 50m to the village centre (⚑: San Michele Arcangelo) and turn left on a wide track. Walking parallel with the road, you leave the village, pass the cemetery and join the main road again (**15min**). Now follow it 200m straight on, then turn right on a track descending to a stream, which is crossed by curving right. The track, lined by old oak trees, continues through a meadow towards a watering place for animals. Your ongoing route is about 50m *before* the spring's white concrete troughs (**30min**): a grassy trail, climbing left, to the edge of the woods. Veering right, it ascends steeply southwest in the shade of oaks and beeches. The trail turns left by a little concrete building and reaches a junction 50m further on: take the path climbing straight ahead here, walking south across a meadow. After 10 more minutes you come to a **saddle** east of Monte dell'Eremita

(1295m; **1h**). On the left is a bubbling spring with drinking water, on the right a low concrete building behind which several grassy small trails climb the hillside. Continue on the lowest, most worn trail, which contours along the southwestern side of the mountain. Beyond a stretch through some oaks, the trail fades out in the treeless meadows. Continue climbing over open terrain, veering a little to the right and keeping to the right of a long gully coming up from the valley. You come to a low saddle on the main ridge (**1h35min**), with a wire fence.

With the fence on your right, follow a trail running west, climbing a short way onto the nearly treeless large summit plains. Up here you have a superb panorama: to the west and south you look down into the deep valley of river Nera, to the north to neighbouring Monte Coscerno, and to the east towards the high Monti Sibillini, which are covered with snow for much of the year. The flat

81

On Monte dell'Eremita

mountain summit soon divides into two ridges, a northern one with Monte di Civitella (1565m) and a southern one, which we follow to the highest point of **Monte dell' Eremita** (1546m; **2h**).

From here veer hard left and follow small sheeps' trails for 15 minutes down the bleak slopes in a south-easterly direction, until you come to a gully at the foot of a **protruding rock face** dropping steeply to the east (**2h15min**). Down on the right,

150m away, a **watering-place** with two troughs (drinking water) is visible. *The Variation from Monte San Vito comes up here.*

Turn to the left to follow a path contouring the southern slopes of Monte dell'Eremita. Gently climbing, you cross two stream beds and then come back to your outgoing route above a **third gully** (**2h45min**). From here retrace your steps to **Gavelli** (**3h45min**).

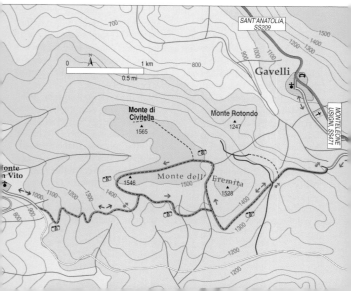

Walk 14: FROM SANT'EUTIZIO THROUGH VALLE CASTORIANA

See photograph page 26
Distance/time: 15km; 5h
Grade: moderate; ascent of 670m
Equipment: as pages 46-47
Refreshments: bar at the road

below Campi Vecchio
How to get there: 🚌 to Sant'Eutizio (Car tour 5 at 89km); 🚌 Mon-Sat 3 buses from Borgo Cerreto to Norcia via Piedivalle; 10min walk to start

This hike skirts the edge of Valle Castoriana, a pleasant side-valley branching off the Valnerina. From the 5th century onwards Christian hermits retreated here to meditate, like Sant' Eutizio who came all the way from Syria. Today a feeling of peace and quiet still permeates the valley, with it deciduous forests, poplar-lined meadows, historic villages and churches. Higher up, on the foothills of the Monti Sibillini, the landscape becomes rougher and lonelier. Except for an earnest-looking shepherd with his animals (maybe armed with an old gun as protection against wolves), you will hardly ever meet anyone up here.

Start at Sant'Eutizio Abbey (680m): follow the valley road uphill to the hamlet of Valle (15min). Opposite a fountain on the right, go left between houses for 50m, then turn right on a trail (⌐: San Fiorenzo). At the next junction, just above the hamlet, turn left, in two minutes passing a square concrete water storage building. Behind it follow an old pilgrims' trail, climbing north along the eastern hillside. Within 15 minutes you reach the remote medieval hermit's chapel of San Fiorenzo (45min).

Turn sharp left 20m behind the chapel (in front of the benches). This initially stony path climbs gently along the southeastern slope, with fine views above the Valle Castoriana. Join a track (55min), which rises more steeply. To the east the barren ridge of the Monte Lungo comes into sight. After about 10 minutes the gradient eases, and the track runs along the edge of a conifer wood on the left. Around 100m before the end of the wood take a trail branching off right and walk through a grassy hollow to the flat saddle (1205m; 1h30min) between Monte Moricone (1429m) and Monte Lungo (1252m). Continue straight ahead on the track to the right of a rest area with

wooden tables. Curving uphill to the right, you emerge on the long (lungo) grassy ridge of Monte Lungo. With far-reaching views over the cornfields of the Acquaro Valley towards the barren Monti Sibillini, follow the trail across the flat summit ridge to its southern end. Then descend a short way, to a signposted pass, where you meet a track coming up left from the Acquaro valley (2h05min). Cross this (⌐: Campi Vecchio; red and white waymarks) and take a path leading over a little hill. Meeting another track, follow it straight on, along the northern hillside of Monte Macchialunga. After a stretch of gentle descent through a beech wood and hazelnut wood, you come to a field by an enclosure on the left. (Watch out for dogs here!) Climb a short way along the edge of the field, to the saddle (2h30min) between Monte Macchialunga (1274m) and Monte Monticello (1305m). From here carefully follow the red and white waymarks south downhill on an initially-faint path. As you descend through oak woods into the valley of Campi, the path becomes clearer but occasionally very stony. About 20 minutes from the saddle, the path veers sharp left (east). Then, beyond a stream, it joins a

83

wide track, by the ruins of **Madonna del Condotto (3h05min)**. Climb a few metres straight ahead, between the church and a spring (drinking water), onto the embankment, then follow a flat path to the right, contouring the hillside with fine views. Rounding a bend, you enter the old village of **Campi Vecchio**, leaning against steep slopes high above Valle Castoriana. Keeping to the upper village lane, you reach the main **church of Sant'Andrea (3h25min)**, a pleasant place for a break, with a view down to the valley bottom.

In front of the church go down the steps to the right, then walk over to the Campi Vecchio access road. Follow this downhill. At crossroads near the church of Sant'Antonio continue straight on; then, in front of a shrine with a Madonna, turn left, down to the Norcia/Preci valley road. Cross this, pass Bar-Alimentari Onori on the left, and after 30m come to another shrine with a blue Madonna. Turn right on a track, dip down to cross a stream, then climb a short way up to the Romanesque church of **San Salvatore (3h40min;** interesting frescoes but seldom open).

Just 30m to the left of the church you cross the Norcia/Preci road again and follow a track north into fields. Take the second left turn, in front of a little iron cross, to continue west on a flat farm track — with a good view back towards Campi Vecchio. Beyond a right-hand bend you climb a short way through oak wood to an Y-fork. Go left here (50m to the right is the church of Madonna della Croce). After a steep 10-minute ascent, a flat stretch takes you through gorse brush with views down into the valley. Veering right into the side-valley of Fosso di Stigni, the trail narrows to a lovely path. You cross the ditch on an overgrown **footbridge (4h30min)** dating from medieval times, then climb a short way left along the hillside. Once more descending, on an old, partly cobbled mule trail, you pass a ruined chapel and reach the hamlet of **Acquaro (4h50min)**. Walk between the houses for 50m; then, at a larger building, turn left down steps. At house No 4 walk a few paces to the left, then go right, through an arch. Continue past here on a path for five minutes, then descend back to **Sant'Eutizio (5h)**.

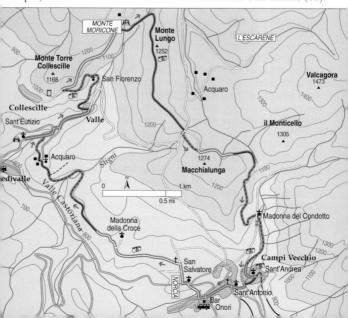

Walk 15: ABOVE THE ROOFTOPS OF GUBBIO

Distance/time: 8km; 2h30min
Grade: easy; ascent/descent of 530m
overall. In wet conditions *take care*
on the narrow path along the steep
western slope of Monte Asciano.
Equipment: as pages 46-47
Refreshments: bar-trattoria in
Coppo (not always open)
How to get there: 🚗 to Gubbio
(base for Car tour 6); 🚌 to Gubbio
(several buses daily, either from
Perugia or from Fossato di Vico on
the Ancona/Rome railway line)

Each year during the 'Corsa dei Ceri' on May 15th, *i matti* ('the madmen') of Gubbio, carrying a huge heavy wooden candle, storm up the winding track to the basilica of Sant'Ubaldo in three competing groups. The last part of this short walk follows the pine- and cypress-lined route the runners take to the church of the town's patron saint. But before we reach Sant'Ubaldo, the barren ridges of Monte Asciano and Monte Ingino offer panoramic views over the surrounding hills towards the distant central Apennines. The medieval town of Gubbio is one of the few places where unspoilt nature can be found just near the *centro storico*.

Starting out at the **Piazza Grande** in **Gubbio**, in front of the superb medieval town hall (**Palazzo dei Consoli**). Leave the square to the east on Via XX Settembre, which leads to the 12th-century church of **San Marziale** at the edge of the *centro storico*. Past the church, fork left on an ascending side-road (⌐: S. Gerolamo; red and white waymarks, Sentiero 253), to leave the old town via the ancient **Porta Vehia**). After five minutes, where the road bends right in front of a rest area, you look north towards a rocky valley. Fork sharp left 150m past the bend, on a path which veers right and climbs the hillside, with views back to Gubbio's old walls. After some steep zigzags to the left you come back to the road, which you follow straight ahead past Stations of the Cross to the monastery of **San Gerolamo** (**30min**).
Turn sharp left in front of the church on a gently-climbing track, initially

heading west and then (after five minutes), east. The track runs alongside a fence, then ends at a gate (**45min**). Turn sharp left 20m *before* the gate, to follow a path up the southwestern slopes of Monte d'Asciano. Climb steeply for 10 minutes, after which the path flattens out and veers right, around the hillside. *Take care* in wet conditions, as this narrow path, covered with foliage, contours the western slopes. You can see Sant'Ubaldo on the far side of the valley. The path curves once more to the right, to come to a signposted crossroads in a hollow sheltered by pine trees. Continue straight uphill (⌐: Coppo). You leave the wood 150m further on (**1h10min**), emerging on a grassy ridge, and the Bar-Trattoria Coppo comes into view 200m ahead — a popular destination for Sunday day-trippers.
Before continuing, a **diversion** to the right takes you steadily up the

85

summit ridge onto bleak **Monte d'Asciano** (893m; **1h30min**), from where you can look down onto Gubbio far below.

Retrace your steps and walk to the Bar Coppo (**1h45min**), then take the road northwest, to a T-junction at the foot of Monte Ingino. From here take a steep narrow path up the northeastern slopes; two zigzags bring you to the summit of **Monte Ingino** (908m) with the scant remains of a **ruined castle**, another fine viewpoint. From here a short trail descends to **Sant'Ubaldo** (**2h10min**). From the basilica walk down the wide winding track lined with cypresses, the route of the Ceri-runners. You quickly reach the edge of **Gubbio**'s *centro storico*, by the **cathedral** and the **ducal palace**. Take the lane down to the left, back to Via XX Settembre and the **Piazza Grande** (**2h30min**).

Gubbio: Training for the Corsa dei Ceri

Walk 16: FROM MIRATOIO TO SASSO DI SIMONE

Distance/time: 15km; 4h30min
Grade: moderate, with an overall ascent/descent of 650m. Orientation is not always easy on the first stretch from Miratoio to Case Barboni.
Note: after rainfall the trails around the Sella di due Sassi become very muddy, in which case it is better to limit yourself to the Short walk.
Equipment: as pages 46-47
Refreshments: Bar at Miratoio (not always open)

How to get there: 🚌 to Miratoio (the 103km-point on Car tour 7); no public transport
Short walk to Sasso di Simone: 6km; 2h; easy. About 4km east of Miratoio (just before Petrella Massana) the road to Sestino passes a car park with hiking map. Take the uphill lane here, to hamlet of **Case Barboni** (10min). Follow the main walk from the 1h20min-point to Sasso di Simone; return the same way.

In the Montefeltro mountains on the border with Tuscany we find the Riserva Naturale del Sasso di Simone. This is a remote, sparsely-populated region with little villages and old farms surrounded by wide meadows with abundant wild flowers. Two striking, isolated table-topped mountains with rocky limestone cliffs rise up from the green woods, and one of them is the goal of this walk. While Simoncello (1221m) is not all that to easy to climb, an easy mule trail rises onto neighbouring Sassi di Simone (1209m). The trail was built in the 16th century, when the powerful Medicis from Florence built a castle on the flat summit (of which no traces can be found today). On the southern slopes of the range the ground is covered with large meadows, while to the north there are dense deciduous forests. In between, the lunar-like landscape of the *calanchi* suddenly opens up — deeply eroded earthen slopes, the barren soil in hues of grey and red.

Starting point is the centre of **Miratoio**. Coming from the direction of Pennabilli, to the right of the main road there's a fountain with a little stone stela. Take the cobbled ramp opposite the fountain, going uphill across a surfaced track; then turn right on an earthen track which contours the steep rocky hillside north of the village (🚩: Banditella, Sasso di Simone, Sentiero 17). After five minutes curving left around the slope, you pass a pond for watering cattle on the right. Beyond it, in front of a field, turn right and follow an initially-muddy trail uphill along the grassy ridge coming down Simoncello. After 300m uphill, where an earthen stretch begins to climb more steeply to the left (this will be your return route), turn right on a path (*not waymarked*). This path

heads right and is less steep. It contours the upper end of an eroded hollow, crossing a ditch by an isolated oak. Behind the oak the way curves left and rises up the grassy slopes. The hamlet of Poggio Mazzolo comes into sight ahead (**30min**). Following small cattle trails gently uphill, you pass two more ponds on the right and continue southeast through a gate in the fencing. A few minutes later you meet a farm track coming up from Poggio Mazzolo (**45min**).
Follow this 200m downhill towards Poggio Mazzolo. When you come to a small wooden signpost on the right (and an animal gate running across the track), climb a trail to the left for 50m, onto a saddle. From here descend a fading trail, veering a little to the left for 500m, down to the

87

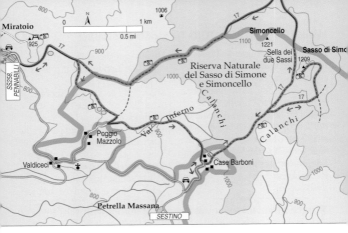

remote valley of **Val'Inferno**. From here the cliffs of Simoncello and Sasso di Simone appear in the northeast (**1h**).

At the bottom of the valley you cross two streams on stepping stones; the stream beds are strewn with debris and rocks. On the opposite side climb the steep slopes at the left of a little wood. The path becomes clearer and flattens out as you follow a ridge with an eroded, red-hued valley on your left. Keep your eyes open for a sunken trail leading off to the right; this takes you in five minutes to the **Case Barboni** (**1h20min**), where a lot of (harmless) dogs are likely to be running about. *(The Short walk joins here.)*

From here take a grassy trail which starts at the right of the uppermost house (red and white waymarks of Route 61). This climbs northeast in a good five minutes to a low hill with a small mast. After passing a

gate, turn a little to the right and follow a path uphill over barren soil. You soon come to a moon-like landscape of furrowed steep slopes, the **Calanchi**. The path (⌐: Sasso di Simone 0.35 h) skirts the edge of the verge. The isolated table mountain of Sasso di Simone comes into sight ahead, soon joined by Simoncello to the west. Keep right after a short steep descent. Five minutes later you come to a Y-fork (**1h40min**). Before continuing left back to Miratoio, take a **diversion** to the right, to Sasso di Simone. The path (the red and white waymarked Route 17), veers a little to the right and runs above the *calanchi,* then descends for some minutes to a stream (dry most of the year). It then rises again over rocky terrain and through blocks of stone. Now the rock face of Sasso di Simone rise in front of you like a castle. You come to the foot of the cliffs at the eastern edge of the mountain (**2h**), where you go through a fence and then follow the the old mule trail around the eastern hillside and up

towards the flat summit. On the way up, you come to a board in the shade of a little wood, with a copper relief depicting the one-time castle of the Medicis. From here take a path to the left, which leads within five more minutes onto the flat grassy plateau on top of **Sasso di Simone** (1209m; **2h15min**). From the western edge you have a lovely view to neighbouring Monte Simoncello (1221m).

Retrace your steps back to the junction at the 1h40min-point (**2h40min**), where you turn sharp right. From here all the way back to Miratoio, follow the red and white waymarks of Route 17. This runs north along the ridge, with views towards the two table mountains. Climbing in the shade of oak and beech trees, you reach a saddle, the **Sella dei due Sassi** (**3h05min**).

Beyond the saddle take the woodland trail to the left, descending northwest. In just under 15 minutes from the saddle, fork sharp left on another trail, this one narrower and flat (**3h20min**). For another good 15 minutes you enjoy the shade of deciduous trees before emerging on an open ridge with a few pines and a a superb panorama. Take the small path descending west along the ridge. Looking back, the twin mountains come into view again, standing above steep and deeply-eroded slopes. Keeping always to the barren hilltop, head downhill, always with far-reaching views, until you join your outward ascent route. Now retrace your steps to **Miratoio** (**4h30min**).

Landscape near Case Barboni. The stones mark the boundary between Tuscany and the Marche

Walk 17: ABOVE FURLO GORGE

Distance/time: 17km; 5h15min
Grade: moderate-tough, with an overall ascent/descent of around 700m; orientation is quite easy.
Equipment: as pages 46-47; take sufficient drinking water with you
Refreshments: bar, restaurant at Furlo; none en route
How to get there: 🚗 to Furlo (Car Tour 7 at the 172km-point). The 🚌 on the Acqualagna–Fano/Urbino line stops at the Albergo Birra al Pozza about 1km west of Furlo hamlet (Line 24; hourly buses Mon-Sat; www.adriabus.eu)
Shorter circuit: 11km; 3h20min; easy-moderate, with 350m of ascent/descent. 🚗 to **Pagino Castello**: coming from Acqualagna on the expressway, take the first exit after the tunnel, signed to Calmazzo. Keep right to join the country road to Calmazzo, pass a bus stop and fork left on a small road signposted for Pagino Castello some 3km away. **Start** at **Pagino Castello** by the cypress-shaded **cemetery**. Follow the wide track running straight ahead, with the cemetery on your right. Some 50m along, in front of a

shrine, turn left (south) on a smaller, level track. This easy route passes an overgrown stone house and reaches a long building called **Case Preci** (**50min**), where it ends. From here take the path straight ahead (it begins at the left of a spring with drinking water, by some fig trees; red and white waymarks of Route 440). The pleasant path curves right and contours the hillside, with views down into the Gola di Furlo. The sound of road traffic comes up from the valley as you walk through typical Mediterranean vegetation with pines and holm oaks. At a Y-fork in front of a **single cypress**, go right; follow the main walk from the **1h40min-point** to the **Rifugio del Furlo**. Then walk right uphill on the main track for five minutes before forking right on a smaller track with an iron barrier. Some 50m behind the barrier you meet your outgoing route: retrace your step to to **Pagino Castello**.
Walking map: Carta Turistica Monti del Furlo (1:15,000), Topos Edizioni Fano, on sale at the bar of the Albergo Furlo in Furlo.

This walk runs through the mountains above a deep gorge, the Gola di Furlo, not far south of the picturesque town of Urbino. One of the highlights is a superb viewpoint — on the broken nose of Mussolini. The dictator had his huge portrait carved out of the limestone rock; it was later blown apart by the Partisans. Below you, the turquoise-blue waters of the Candigliano wind their way through steep rocky cliffs. On the stony southern slopes exposed to the sun there is luxuriant evergreen vegetation, with many cypresses and even some wild cedars.

Start out at the **Albergo Antico Furlo**. Walk behind the barrier and follow the road through the gorge. The **Candigliano River** is dammed to a narrow lake with greenish water reflecting steep lime cliffs. After about half an hour's walking the road goes through a small tunnel (pierced by the Romans for the Via Flaminia in the year 76 under Emperor Vespasian). You then pass

a small dam and the road barrier at the eastern side of the gorge. About 200m further on, at the **Passo Furlo**, the road widens out for a parking area on the left (180m; **45min**).
At the start of the parking area turn sharp left behind a white-brown 'Passo Furlo' road sign and take the path on the bank (⌐: Terrazza del Furlo, red/white waymarks, Route

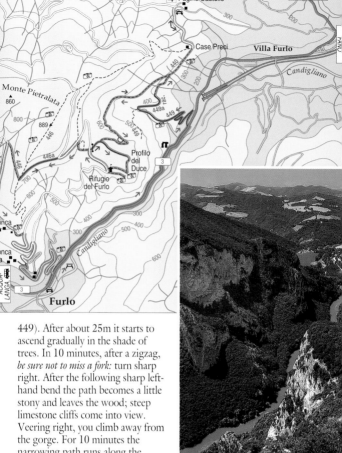

449). After about 25m it starts to
ascend gradually in the shade of
trees. In 10 minutes, after a zigzag,
be sure not to miss a fork: turn sharp
right. After the following sharp left-
hand bend the path becomes a little
stony and leaves the wood; steep
limestone cliffs come into view.
Veering right, you climb away from
the gorge. For 10 minutes the
narrowing path runs along the
eastern slope of a side-valley with a
small stream — which you then
cross by stepping stones. Steep short
zigzags then take you back down to
the **bed of the stream** (370m;
1h20min).
Route 449 goes off left here, but
you now turn sharp right, crossing
the stream once more. Your small
path, also marked with red/white
stripes (Route 449a/raccordo),
continues to the east. Initially it rises
a little, then descends slightly,
swinging left around the hillside.
Turn right at the foot of a steep
rocky slope, where the path becomes
stony. But after a short climb it's
earthen underfoot, running level

between pines. The sound of road
traffic comes up from the valley. At a
single cypress you join a wider path
(386m; 1h40min). *(The shorter
circuit joins here.)*
Turn sharp left (◾: Pian di Maglie,
red/white way marks, route 440).
The path widens to a trail and climbs
the eastern slopes of Monte Pietralata. Then it curves left and narrows
to a path again, now leading
through blackberry bushes and into
a wood, where you pass a little cave
on the right (**2h10min**). Past the
cave the path circles to the right
around the hillside, then runs gently

91

up across a slope with bushes and holm oaks. To the east, beyond the hills, the coastline near Fano comes into view. At the highest point in the path you come to track with an **iron barrier** (**2h25min**).

Some 50m in front of the barrier turn sharp left on a grassy trail *(no waymarks)*. This descends slightly, then veers a little to the right and rises between conifers. Ten minutes from the barrier, where the trail ends, climb 30m to the right through the edge of the woods, to a clearing. Cross half-left, to a path leading into shrubby woods. After 50m the path leaves the little wood and offers a view down to the Gola di Furlo. Descending more steeply, you step onto a rocky promontory, the **Profilo del Duce** (**2h40min**). From Mussolini's broken nose you enjoy a splendid view across the deep gorge towards the Apennines, with Monte Catria and Monte Nerone.

From here go right on a stony trail with a guard rail (red and white waymarks), which leads within five minutes to the **Rifugio del Furlo** (usually locked). A **diversion** to the left leads to another superb outlook (a good 10 minutes walk there and back): behind the building take the flat path to the left, then ignore a path forking left uphill. You come to a terrace overlooking the river Candigliano far below, between steep limestone cliffs.

Back at the Rifugio del Furlo (**3h**), take the wide track climbing to the right behind the building. Opposite a smaller track on the right with an iron barrier, turn left on a path (red and white waymarks). *(But for the Short circuit go right here.)* Forking left at two junctions, then veering to the right uphill through woods, the waymarks lead you back to the main track (**3h15min**).

Follow the main track to the left for another five minutes, to a clear right-hand bend, where you leave the track and continue straight ahead on a trail. After 10 minutes this level trail comes to an **open promontory**, where waymarked Route 446 coming down from Monte Pietralata joins your route (**3h35min**). Keeping to the red- and white-waymarked Route 446, descend to the right. Ten minutes from the promontory you meet a track, which you follow to the left (south), with the occasional view to the Apennines. After a left-hand bend you walk through a bit of woods with the hidden ruins of **Spelonca Alta** hamlet on the right. Beyond the ruins you come to a rock face with a line of cypresses on the left. The track veers left again at this point (**4h05min**); on the right there is a little square concrete water storage building and, a few paces ahead, some pretty cedars stand against a backdrop of the limestone cliffs of Furlo Gorge.

At the concrete building head down the steep slope for 30m, to another small path. This descends to the left through a section of wood with more cedar trees, to meet the wide track used before from the Rifugio del Furlo. This takes you downhill in curves — a bit dull, but with some lovely views down into the gorge with its steep cliffs. At the second sharp left-hand bend, where tarmac comes underfoot (**4h25min**), take a track to the right towards private property. Then, after 30m, go left on a path through cypresses, down to the entrance gate to a villa. Go right here and then left almost immediately, down to the nearby tarred road. You now have to follow this road for the rest of the walk. (Short-cuts shown on the recommended map were completely overgrown at time of writing.) Passing the few houses of **Spelonca Bassa** (**4h40min**), the small road heads down through three more wide bends (and more good views), to the village of **Furlo** (**5h15min**).

Walk 18: ON MONTE NERONE NEAR PIOBBICO

Photograph page 31
Distance/time: 12km; 3h50min
Grade: moderate in length and
height gain (ascent/descent of
350m), but you must be sure-
footed to cross the rocky slope
at the 2h45min-point. Orientation is not always easy along
the middle section of the walk.
At several points a stream has to
be crossed: depending on the
water level you probably have
to remove your hiking boots.
Equipment: as pages 46-47;
plastic sandals useful for stream
crossings
How to get there: 🚗 see Car
tour 6 at the 58km-point (limited
parking by the km34 road marker at
Case le Brecce). 🚌 Acqualagna/
Apecchio/Città di Castello line (Line
23), Mon-Sat 3 to 5 buses, Info:
www.adriabus.eu; alight at Case le
Brecce
Refreshments: none en route
Short walk: 5km; 1h30min; easy,
with 150m ascent/descent. 🚗 as
above, but park at km34 III (the
yellow signposted track into the
Vitoschio Valley). **Start** by following the main road towards Piobbico

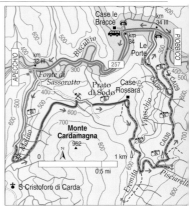

for 5min. In front of the new road
bridge across Biscubio go right, past
some sheds on your left (CAI Route
29). Beyond them, take a path up
right, climbing the barren slopes to a
rocky ridge, with a lovely view west
into Vitoschio Valley. Follow the
path south along the ridge for a
good 5min, into a wood where CAI
30 branches off right. From here
follow the main walk from the
3h10min-point, back to km34 III.
Walking map: Carta dei Sentieri
Monte Nerone, 1:25,000, available

O n this hike we explore the varied, sometimes wild landscape
on the northern slopes of Monte Nerone. Winding streams
with little waterfalls, rocky limestone cliffs and sombre little
woods accompany us through the remote valleys of Fosso
dell'Eremita, Fosso Pisciarello and Rio Vitoschio. The latter is
particularly idyllic, with colourful butterflies and shiny blue
dragonflies buzzing through the fresh green above the clear
waters of the stream.

Starting point is the group of
houses called **Case le Brecce** on the
north side of the Piobbico/Apecchio
road at the little km34 marker
(limited parking). First walk just
under 2km along the road through
Biscubio Valley, heading upstream
towards Apecchio. Although the
road is tarred, this is not a boring
stretch, since steep red-hued cliffs
rise above the winding river.

Reaching the km32 III marker, you
come to the tiled mineral spring of
Fonte di Sassorotto; the water is
said to ease digestive problems.
Just in front of the fountain, turn left
on a wide track (**25min**). At the
junction 200m further on, take the
smaller fork to the right. This
steadily gains height on the western
side of the Fosso del Molino valley.
Rocky cliffs rise to your right. Some

93

20 minutes from Fonte Sassorotto take a path off left, to the **ruin of a house**. From the shoulder to the left of the ruin **vertical rock cleft** comes into view, where the Molino steam drops down 30m into a little pool. The ongoing path continues to the right of the ruin, after 100m coming to **a ruined watermill**. Climb the slope 5m to the right, and carefully follow a narrow path over bedrock. This leads to a rocky stream bed, the Fosso del Molino, which you cross at the upper end of the cleft you saw earlier (**55min**).

Past the stream bed, follow a path left up the hillside. After around 10 minutes it flattens out below thin beech trees. In another 10 minutes you join a trail, keeping straight ahead. The trail then descends, becomes clearer and veers right through woods. Then it bends left to a T-junction facing an derelict gravel quarry (**1h30min**). Turn right on a wide track and climb 10 minutes to a Y-fork. Go left, onto the overgrown meadows of **Prati di Sodo**. With views down into the Biscubio Valley, ascend the grassy slopes to a derelict farm seen ahead, **Case Rossara** (**1h50min**).

Turn right in front of the ruin and follow a faint trail 100m at the right of the valley. Past a little pond on the left (dry in summer) walk to the edge of the woods, where you find a clearer trail. Follow this to the left. After five minutes the trail narrows to a path contouring the hillside high above the Rio Vitoschio. A promontory a good 20 minutes from Case Rossara gives a superb outlook towards limestone pinnacles rising from the grassy slopes ahead. The path then descends to the bottom of the **Fosso dell'Eremita**, one of two sources feeding the Vitoschio (**2h 20min**). Follow the stream for 50m; then, when the path starts climbing, cross left over the stream on stepping stones. (Ten minutes straight on there's a pretty little waterfall.)

Over the stream, cross an overgrown meadow and walk 50m downstream. Beyond a line of bushes, you'll find a clear forest path waymarked with some faded red spots. This circles to the right along the wooded slope and descends a short way to another stream, the **Fosso Pisciarello**, the second source of Rio Vitoschio. The path keeps beside the stream bed for 100m, then climbs to the right of it for three minutes, to another small path, where you go left. Returning to the Pisciarello, walk another 50m upstream to a junction *(easily missed)*. Your ongoing route crosses the stream to the left here, but first walk ahead for 100m, at the right of the stream, to a lovely **little waterfall** (**2h35min**).

From the stream the path rises steeply for 10 minutes. Leaving the wooded valley, it veers left to a stretch of **sloping, rocky ground**, where *care is needed*. To the west you have a nice view down into the valley you crossed earlier.

At a **signposted junction** three minutes past the rocky slope, follow the red- and white-waymarked CAI Route 30 to the left (**2h50min**; ⌐: Le Porte). The trail descends through woods, then runs along the barren hillside with views to the Case Rossara on the far side of the Vitoschio Valley. Back in the woods, you descend to a junction (**3h10min**), where you ignore CAI Route 29 straight ahead and turn sharp left with CAI30. A stony path takes you down to the bottom of the **Vitoschio Valley**, where you follow the watercourse downstream (crossing several times). The valley, blocked to the north by steep rocks, seems to have no exit, but suddenly the trail leads between two almost-adjacent **rock towers: Le Porte**. Then a track takes you north in 10 minutes to the Piobbico/Apecchio road, which you follow five minutes to the left, back to **Case le Brecce** (**3h50min**).

Walk 19: ON MONTE NERONE NEAR PIANELLO

Distance/time: 13km; 4h
Grade: moderate-strenuous; 550m of ascent. You must be surefooted for the stony path between Pieia and Cerreto; the first part of the walk needs care with orientation; well waymarked from Pieia to Cerreto.
Equipment: as pages 46-47; some very stony trails, so hiking boots are strongly recommended.
Refreshments: only in Pianello
How to get there: 🚗 to Massa (Car tour 6 at 40km); 🚌 from Pianello to Massa (Line 53, Cagli–Massa Ponte Trella), Mon–Sat at 9.24, 14.24, 18.20; Info: www.adriabus.

eu ; buses stop in the lower part of Pianello, in front of the bar.
Variation (Circuit): 11km; 3h45min; moderate (ascent/descent of 450m). Follow the main walk to **Fondarca** (2h10min-point), then turn right on the red- and white-waymarked CAI20. In 5min you return to your outgoing route and retrace your steps. But 15min from Pieia, keep straight ahead on the main track. It rises to a saddle, veers left and runs along the southwestern side of Monte Carpinelo. Again meeting your outgoing route, follow it back to Massa.

This second hike along the slopes of Monte Nerone leads once more into unspoilt mountains. Near Massa you walk through gentle countryside with meadows, pastures and deciduous forests, but near the remote village of Pieia steep limestone cliffs suddenly rise up from the rocky slopes. The karst depression of Fondarca, 15 minutes east of Pieia, encircled by high rock faces, is a very striking sight; it was probably a Stone Age settlement.

The **starting point** is the village of **Massa** 3km northwest of Pianello. In the centre of Massa, the road to Serravalle describes a right-hand bend when coming from Pianello: take the cobbled lane here, ascending steeply through the houses. At the uppermost end of the village you come to a track. Follow this straight on to two houses on the right, built with reddish stone and numbered 104 and 108. Turn off right here, passing between the two buildings

and curving left on a grassy path (occasional red and white waymarks). At the following junction, keep to the path straight ahead, which climbs through a thin forest, veers right along the edge of a field and rejoins the main Massa/Pieia track (**25min**).
Follow this track uphill for three minutes. Then, 100m past a sharp bend to the left, turn right on a stony trail, diagonally ascending the southern slopes of Monte Carpinelo.

After 100m the trail narrows to a pleasant path. Where the waymarked path forks left (**40min**), continue straight ahead. Around five minutes later you step onto a treeless slope offering far-reaching views to the southwest. Follow the upper edge of the meadow for 100m, then climb a small path to the left, up through gorse and to an open ridge, with

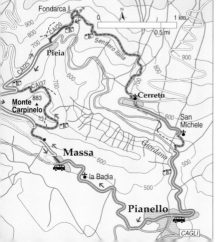

95

panoramic views across the valley of Cerreto towards Monte Nerone. Now follow a faint path to the left, going uphill along the southwestern side of the grassy ridge, to a flat **saddle below Monte Carpinelo**, where you meet the waymarked route again (810m; **1h05min**). This waymarked route follows the upper path to the right and leads to the edge of a thin oak wood. Then a narrow but clear path, occasionally waymarked in red, takes you down the eastern hillside for 10 minutes, to a grassy saddle, where you turn hard left. A pleasant path with views towards the limestone rocks above Pieia leads you down to the main Massa/Pieia track (**1h25min**). Follow this downhill through a lovely verdant valley, to the village of **Pieia** (655m; **1h45min**).

In front of the village fountain, go up some steps to the left; then, past a small area for playing bowls, follow a path to the right (red and white waymarks of CAI Route 20, plus Sentiero Italia). After a flat stretch along the hillside, the path makes a short but steep climb to a Y-fork. Take the gravel path to the left, continuing steeply uphill to the rock arch shown above, the entrance to the **karst doline of Fondarca**. You leave this unusual site by an opening in the rock at the upper end and then continue 100m, to a steep limestone cliff where a thin jet of water pours down (after rain). Descending a steep gravel path along the foot of the rock face, you come back to the red- and white-
96

waymarked main path (**2h10min**). Turn left here. *(But for the Circuit variation, go right.)*

For the rest of the hike you follow the red- and white-waymarked Sentiero Italia, which describes a large curve to the right, all the way undulating along the western hillside. After an exposed stretch with view back to Pieia, you climb 30m up a rocky stream bed. Five minutes later you head downhill along grassy slopes. Now, *do not miss* a right-hand bend (**2h25min**). Beyond this bend the path starts climbing again. Later it circles to the right above a large, steeply-sloping **eroded section** (**2h45min**), before descending into a bleak valley, where you cross a stream bed (usually dry). Over the stream bed the path rises again, then levels out for a short way, with long views over the valley of Pieia. Gaining a little height again, you eventually come to the meadows of **Cerreto** (674m; **3h05min**).

In the village, in front of the little church, go down some steps to the right, then cross the road leading uphill to Cerreto. Near a house on the right, turn left downhill on a path. Come back to the road, follow it to the left out of the village for about 250m, until you come to a sharp bend to the right. Continue straight ahead here on a surfaced track. A good five minutes' walk takes you down to the little Romanesque church of **San Michele** (**3h30min**). From the meadow in front of the church turn a little to the left, on a path with a yellow sign. It zigzags downhill to the Pieia/Pianello road, which sees little traffic. Follow this to the left along the slopes above the Giordano stream for 15 minutes, to **Pianello** (**4h**). From here return to Massa by bus or, if no bus is due, walk the 3km back to Massa.

Walk 20: AROUND FONTE AVELLANA MONASTERY ON MONTE CATRIA

See also photograph page 32
Distance/time: 10km; 3h15min
Grade: moderate, with an overall ascent/descent of 480m; orientation needs care in some places
Equipment: as pages 46-47
How to get there: 🚌 to Forchetta Pass (Car tour 6 just before the 94km-point); no public transport

Refreshments: bar near monastery
Shorter walk: 8km; 2h30min; easy, with 360m ascent/descent: omit the diversion to Monte Mura.
Hiking maps: Kompass No 664 (Gubbio-Fabriano) or No 675 (Sentiero Europeo E1 Tratto Umbro); Carta dei Sentieri Monte Catria, 1:25,000, Club Alpino Pesaro

Up to a few decades ago the medieval monastery of Fonte Avellana in remote Monte Catria could only be reached on foot. Even today this seems the most appropriate way to approach this beautiful site, where monks of the Camaldule Order still live, far away from the modern world. The walk to the monastery leads through shady forests and across large meadows with abundant wild flowers in early summer and gives superb views to the steep and rocky eastern side of the huge Monte Catria massif (1701m).

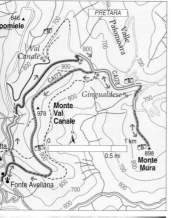

Starting point is the **pass of Forchetta** (782m), the highest point on the Frontone/Fonte Avellana road (small car park). From here follow the road 30m to the north, then turn right on a wide earthen track. Follow this for a 10 minutes, initially climbing gently through woods, then walking almost level, with views west to steeply-sloping Monte Catria. Branch off right, go round a barrier and follow a smaller track waymarked with red and yellow stripes uphill under beeches. After three minutes you come to a sloping meadow with a good view to Monte Catria. Here the trail veers right onto a low ridge, which you follow south for 50m. Then turn left on a forest trail running northeast along the flank of Monte Val Canale (**15min**).

The small track rises slightly through beech wood for about 15 minutes. Then, leaving the forest, it fades away on a meadow, offering far views towards the Adriatic coast. Continue straight ahead on a faint grassy path for 200m, then take a farm track on your left. Within three minutes you descend to a larger

Monte Val Canale

97

track (**35min**). Go right, past three troughs from a spring on the right. Follow the wide track contouring the northeastern side of the mountain range. You come to a second left-hand bend with a **dry drinking trough** (**45min**) standing 50m to the right in the meadow; here your ongoing route to Fonte Avellana forks right.

Before continuing, however, first divert straight ahead for five minutes along the main track: this takes you to the **saddle** 50m above the concrete spring of **Fonte delle Gingualdese** (788m; **50min**), where a track rising from the Petrara Valley comes in on the left. Some tree-shaded benches make this a fine spot for a break. You look out across a flowery meadow towards remote, uninhabited mountains, with the prominent massif of Monte Catria (1701m) and adjacent Corno di Catria, with its steep rocky cliffs, to the south.

From here the grassy shoulder of Monte Mura mountain to the south can easily be climbed. Follow a faint trail across the sloping meadows, passing to the right of a rounded concrete wall, and onto the flat summit, where some dark holly bushes stand like silent guardians. Though not very high, barren **Monte Mura** (898m; **1h15min**) offers a superb panoramic outlook over the surrounding mountains. Retrace your steps down to the **saddle** above **Fonte delle Gingualdese** and from there follow the track for five minutes, back to the bend with the **dry drinking trough** (**1h35min**).

Here you leave the track, to continue straight uphill on a goats' trail. Climb the eastern slope of Monte Val Canale all the way to the top (occasional red and white waymarks of CAI Route 73). Follow a more or less flat path south along the narrow and precipitous summit ridge, with far-reaching views (frequent red/white waymarks). Keep to the left of the edge of the wood. Slightly ascending, you crest the **highest point of Monte Val Canale** (978m; **2h**).

About five minutes later the path descends away from the top of the ridge into a thin forest. *Take care here* not to miss the waymarked turn-off left. Your small path climbs back to the top of the ridge. Follow an old fence and go through a gate in a newer fence. Keep to the left side of the ridge, which drops steeply to the east. The monastery of Fonte Avellana comes into view. Again the path starts to descend away from the ridge. After 50m in the woods, *leave* the waymarked route: branch off left on a small path leading back into open grassland. This path contours to the right of the southernmost hillock of the summit ridge until it reaches the edge of a low forest, where it fades away. Descend south now across the treeless meadow for 200m — pathless — until you meet a clear path with red/white waymarks, swinging around the south side of the ridge (**2h40min**).

Follow this towards Fonte Avellana, go right at a fork three minutes later and descend through woods for five minutes, to the start of a small track. It takes you gently downhill, curving left through a valley. After passing a gate keep to the left of a restored old stone house, take a stepped trail down to **Fonte Avellana Monastery** (**3h**).

Leave Fonte Avellana the way you arrived. A good five minutes from the monastery, at a clear Y-fork, leave your original route and turn left uphill on a red/yellow waymarked path. This climbs through an oak forest, goes through a gate (which opens on its left side) and arrives back at the starting point on **Forchetta Pass** (**3h15min**).

Walk 21: ON MONTE CUCCO

Distance/time: 12km; 3h45min
Grade: moderate, with an overall
ascent/descent of 580m; except for
the final 30min the route is well
waymarked in red and white
Equipment: as pages 46-47
Refreshments: Albergo Monte
Cucco; small refuge with bar/restau-
rant on Pian delle Macinare (only
open in high summer)
How to get there: 🚌 to the Albergo
Monte Cucco (Car tour 6 at the
261km-point); no public transport
**Shorter walk, past Monte Cucco
Cave:** 7km; 2h; less strenuous but
more difficult, with 350m of ascent.
The very steep path uphill from
Monte Cucco Cave is only suitable
for surefooted hikers with a head for
heights. Do not walk this stretch in
wet conditions, when the ground is
slippery. **Start the walk** at **Pian del
Monte** (1215m) at the end of the
surfaced road up to Monte Cucco.
Go straight across the meadow to a
trail you can see to the right. This
climbs along the southeastern hillside (Route 2, occasional red and

On the Pian del Monte

white waymarks). Beyond a patch of
wood (**25min**) the trail narrows to a
well-worn balcony path running
close to the precipitous eastern edge
of the slope, to reach the **entrance
to the huge maze of caves** inside
Monte Cucco (1390m; **45min**).
Cool air comes up from the cave.
Going underneath a low rocky arch
on the left, take a narrow stony path,
which rises steeply in short zigzags.
(*Watch for the red and white waymarks!*) Flattening out, this reaches
the junction at the 2h20min-point in
the main walk. Follow the main
walk back to Pian del Monte.

Some 20km east of Gubbio the nature reserve around Monte
Cucco (1566m) offers superb hiking. Small panoramic trails
climb the barren slopes, abundant with wild flowers in spring and
early summer. The lower hillsides have shady deciduous woods
with large beech trees — a fairly rare sight in Mediterranean Italy.
The special feature of the Monte Cucco region is, however,
hidden to the normal hiker: deep inside the mountain there is a
huge labyrinth of karst caves, which can only be explored by well-
equipped speleologists. The shorter, but more difficult variation
of this walk passes the entrance to the cave system.

From the car park below **Albergo
Monte Cucco** (1050m) follow the
track leading north, gently downhill,
into the forest. After about 150m
turn left on CAI Route 1 (⌐: Madre
dei Faggi), which rounds the eastern
slopes in the shade of large beech
trees, without steep ascents. After a
good 15 minutes the forest track
veers left (west) downhill, and ends
in front of a spring, **Fonte Acqua
Fredda** (**25min**). Cross the stream

bed here, then turn right on a red-
and white- waymarked path, which
heads north and undulates along the
mostly-wooded eastern slopes of
Monte Cucco. Ignore CAI Route 17
off to the right (**50min**); instead,
climb steeply up to the left (northwest). From a sloping meadow you
have a good view east. Back in the
beech woods, continue uphill to
some limestone rocks (**1h10min**)
where, from a promontory on the

99

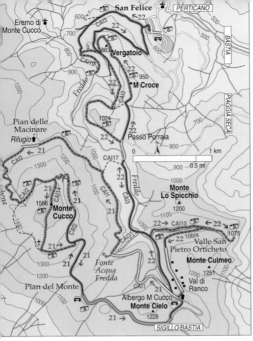

path narrows and contours along the high grassy northern slopes of Monte Cucco with superb views.

At the north-eastern edge of the rise (**2h 20min**) you leave Route 2, which drops steeply. Instead, follow the much easier Route 14 which forks off right at this point. This leads southwest uphill along the barren ridge. Keep on up, past a pre-summit, to the **summit of Monte Cucco**, marked by a cairn. From here you have a 360° view (1568m; **2h35min**).

Now walk south downhill without any clear path across open terrain, to a large **iron cross** standing at the edge of the summit ridge (1435m; **2h55min**). Down on the plain the tiled roofs of Costacciaro come into view. From the cross follow a path veering left around the hillside. Descending more steeply to the east, you meet a clear trail running along the eastern slopes of Monte Cucco (**3h10min**). Follow this down to the flat meadows of **Pian del Ponte** south of Monte Cucco (**3h20min**), a popular starting place for hang-gliders.

From here take the panoramic road heading south for 15 minutes, then turn left on the side-road down to the Val di Ranco settlement. After 50m take the forest trail descending to the left, initially running parallel to the road. In five minutes this takes you back to the car park below **Albergo Monte Cucco** (**3h45min**).

right, you look down to the narrow deeply-etched valley of the Rio Freddo. From here the path winds left round the hillside and descends west along the northern slopes through dark woods strewn with moss-covered boulders. Leaving the woods, you come to the **Pian delle Macinare** (1134m; **1h20min**), a small grassy plain with pleasant places to rest.

Follow the flat main track leading west from the refuge here. After 100m, at the end of a narrow meadow on the left, climb 50m into the wood, to a parallel path, the red-and white-waymarked Route 2. Follow this to the right for five minutes, to a stream bed. Turn left (south) in front of the stream bed, and head steeply up the slope. The path zigzags very steeply up through the sloping wooded depression of **Valrachena**. Some 100m after having left the shade of the thick woods, you come to a junction (**2h05min**). Turn left and follow CAI Route 2 gently uphill. After passing a stand of small beeches the

100

Walk 22: ABOVE THE GORGE OF THE RIO FREDDO

Map opposite
Distance/time: 18km; 5h30min
Grade: strenuous because of the distance; ascent/descent of 700m overall, mostly easy orientation
Equipment: as pages 46-47
Refreshments: bar/restaurant at the Albergo Monte Cucco
How to get there: 🚌 to San Felice (see Car tour 6 at the 109km-point); no public transport. Take the road up to San Felice off the Bastia/Perticano valley road. After 2km it veers left, passes the turn-off left to the church and 200m further on another turn-off right to the northernmost houses. Go 100m ahead and park alongside the unsurfaced road.
Short walks: The main walk, a figure-of-eight, can easily be split into two separate shorter hikes:
1   San Felice — Passo Porraia — San Felice: 10km; 3h35min; moderate, ascent/descent of 550m.

Follow the main walk to the 2h40min-point, then pick it up again at the 4h35min-point.
2   Albergo Monte Cucco — Valle Orticheto — Albergo Monte Cucco: 3.5km; 1h; very easy, with 100m ascent/descent. 🚌 to the Albergo Monte Cucco (Car tour 6 at the 261km-point). From the Albergo follow the main walk from the 3h50min-point: descend CAI Route 3 for around 15 minutes, to the junction at the lower end of Valle San Pietro Orticheto. Then pick up the main walk again at the 3h10min-point, to return uphill to the *albergo*. This short walk can be *extended:* keep to the valley at the 3h30min-point in the main walk. Climb straight on, to the saddle (1075m) between Monte Lo Spicchio and Monte Culmeo, with a far-reaching view to the east (5km; 1h40min; easy, 180m ascent/descent).

T his second walk at Monte Cucco leads through the remote landscape to the east of the mountain which, although only 1566m in height, rises steeply like an Alpine peak from the green woods. We look far down into the Forra di Rio Freddo, where the torrent of the Rio Freddo has cut a narrow gorge into the limestone. We climb two grassy ridges; again, although only around 1000m high, they offer superb panoramic views over the varied mountainous surroundings.

Starting point is the crossroads of tracks in front of the first building in the southern part of **San Felice** (570m). Walk uphill to the right, to the **northern part of the village**, where you follow a lane with a railing between the houses. At the last house, turn left on a trail and climb 100m to a junction. Continue to the right on a slightly overgrown old forest track which rounds the northern slopes of Monte Vergatoio, curving left and gaining height. At a faint junction, keep right, on the main track; this descends a short way, then climbs more steeply. As you round a bend, suddenly the little hermitage of Eremo di Monte Cucco, built against a steep

rockface, comes into view.
At the junction a few paces further on (**25min**), follow the red- and white-waymarked trail to the left (CAI Route 3), which soon narrows to a path. Go left again at the next junction, climbing over stony terrain in the shade of deciduous trees. Leaving the woods, you come to a signposted junction (**40min**). Before continuing left (Route 3) turn right for a **diversion** on Route 19 (also waymarked red and white). The narrow path leads down into the valley of the Rio Freddo. At a clearing you reach the watercourse and can follow it downstream for five minutes, to where it disappears into a rocky cleft (**1h**).

Left: view towards the Eremo di Monte Cucco; below: on Monte Croce

veers left and climbs steeply for 10 minutes alongside a stream bed, still in woods. At the top of the climb the path curves a short way to the left; you meet another path (**2h05min**), which you follow to the right. This good, flat path circles left around the hillside of a nameless elevation (1024m), through woods and little clearings. You come to a little meadow at the **edge of the Rio Freddo Gorge**, a pleasant spot for a break. (Keep back from the steep drop!)

From here rise diagonally up the grassy slope to the **panoramic summit of the mountain** (1024m; **2h30min**). Keeping a little to the right, the path soon starts descending along the western hillside, to the pass of **Passo Porraia** (931m; **2h 40min**). Behind a cattle fence a track comes up from Piaggia Secca. Follow this track down right into the Rio Freddo Valley — which appears more tame from this vantage point. Five minutes from Passo Porraia you cross the usually-dry watercourse and meet a junction. Go

Retracing your steps, return to the junction at the 40min-point (**1h25min**) and follow CAI Route 3 once more. A lovely path takes you gently climbing along the open hillside, to a **saddle** at the foot of Monte Vergatoio, a nice grassy spot with fine views towards Monte Cucco (810m; **1h35min**).

From here Route 3 runs south as a flat trail. At the junction five minutes from the saddle, take the path off to the left. For a 10 minutes you walk along easily in the shade of beech trees. Then the waymarked path

left (still CAI Route 3). Crossing the stony stream bed several times, continue upstream. Ignore CAI Route 31 off right (**3h05min**), beyond which the path becomes steeper. At first walking with the stream bed on the right, then a short way in the bed itself, you come to the **junction of CAI 3 and CAI 10 (3h10min)**. Route 3, which is clearer, crosses the stream to the right and keeps beside the Rio Freddo. But you go left on Route 10. This leads to the east into the lovely tributary of **Valle San Pietro Orticheto**. The path, sometimes ascending over natural stone steps, follows the small watercourse, initially through a shady forest, then through open grassland with views to the barren saddle between Monte Lo Spicchio and Monte Culmeo. Where a flat stony stream bed comes down from the right (**3h30min**), turn sharp right on a path, climbing southwest (CAI Route 10bis). Having crossed a little wood the path veers left round a promontory, offering a nice view to Monte Cucco. Further on, at the edge of the forest settlement Val di Ranco, you join a flat track and follow it

through a wood for a good five minutes, to the **Albergo Monte Cucco** (1050m; **3h50min**). From the parking below the hotel take the wide track running north downhill into the forest. At the junction 150m along, keep right, to follow CAI Route 3 again, descending with the Rio Freddo on your left. Beyond a shady beech forest you meet up with your outgoing route at the junction of CAI 3 and 10 (**4h05min**). Retrace your steps back to the **Passo Porraia** (**4h35min**).

Behind the fencing at the pass follow the flat and grassy trail going off slightly to the right *(no waymarks)*, to contour the eastern hillside of the nameless elevation 1024 m. Some 10 minutes from Passo Porraia you climb a little, to a junction on a saddle. Follow the eroded trail to the right 100m uphill, to come onto a grassy ridge extending far to the north. Follow this, keeping always to the bare summit with its splendid views. You pass the wooden cross of **Monte Croce** (950m) and, 10 minutes later, veer a little to the right, through a bushy hedge and into a hollow. From here rise up again a little, onto **Monte Vergatoio** (883m). Continue straight on, heading down the steep northern slope to a diagonal path. Follow this hard left down along the hillside, after five minutes regaining the **saddle** first reached at the 1h35min-point (810m; **5h**).

Now follow the main track north. It circles to the right around the northern slopes of Monte Vergatoio, with more far-reaching views, then crosses a meadow and descends to a wood. Some 100m into the wood, at a crossroads (**5h15min**), turn sharp left on a skiddy path. This sometimes-overgrown path leads to the junction 100m above San Felice within 10 more minutes. Follow your outgoing route back to **San Felice** (**5h30min**).

Walk 23: THROUGH VALLE SCAPPUCCIA NEAR GENGA

Distance/time: 11km; 3h15min
Grade: easy-moderate, 400m of ascent/descent; easy orientation
Equipment: as pages 46-47
Refreshments: none en route
How to get there: 🚗 to Monticelli (Car tour 6 at the 127km-point).
🚌 Mon-Sat 4 buses from Fabriano via Genga S. Vittore Terme railway station (Line Ancona–Fabriano) to Genga (www.atmaancona.it). From the square in front of the old centre

take the path with wooden railings west to Monticelli where the walk begins (add 1h there and back).
Shorter walk: 8km; 2h40min; easy; 300m ascent/descent. 🚗 to **Capola Villa**, 3km north of Genga. From the upper, western end of the hamlet follow the track 200m north uphill. Follow the main walk from the 40min-point to the 2h55min-point, then turn left on a track (Route 107AG), back to your car.

T he hills and mountains around the spectacular Frasassi Caves have recently come under the protection of the Parco Naturale della Gola della Rossa e di Frasassi. This circuit, near the medieval village of Genga, leads through the northern, less steep part of the nature reserve. We walk through an undulating farmland region typical of the Marche, where rolling hills of corn and sunflower fields alternate with austere forests of oak and pine. The loveliest part of the walk is when we cross Valle Scappuccia, a small stream valley lined by limestone pinnacles.

Start the walk from the little church at the uppermost edge of **Monticelli**. Above the settlement, follow the stony trail climbing straight on from the end of the road (red and white waymarks of Route 107AG). For the first five minutes the gradient is quite steep. Flattening out, the trail crosses a shady wood, then narrows to a path some 20 minutes from Monticelli. Ascending through gorse bushes, you come to a junction in a grassy clearing. Turn right and walk 100m through a stand of conifers, to come to a signposted track (**25min**). Follow this straight ahead (⬆: Valle Scappuccia). The track climbs a short way, veers to the right through a thin wood, and leads down to a junction 200m above the hamlet of **Capola Villa** (**40min**). *(The Shorter walk joins here.)*
Turn sharp left here (red and white waymarks). The track runs left round the hillside, narrows to a path, and (not far past a sharp right-hand bend) drops down to a small meadow, a pleasant place for a

break. Past the meadow veer right, to walk downstream through lovely **Valle Scappuccia**, bordered to the north by some steep limestone cliffs. At the valley's end you suddenly come to a dark rocky cleft: at the end of it the path meets the Genga/ Rocchetta side-road (**1h15min**). Follow the road uphill for just over 500m, to a right-hand bend at the little km17 V marker. Then fork right opposite a shrine with a Madonna, following a track a short way downhill *(no waymarks)*. Within three minutes this brings you to a three-way junction. Take the middle fork, gaining height in the shade of some large oaks. Pass below some low electricity wires and then, 30m further on, veer right, to rise on a grassy trail to a T-junction, where you turn right again. By a stand of oaks between cornfields you pass to the left of an old farmhouse (No 13). Behind the building follow the trail leading up to a track, then go left to the hamlet of **Trivio**. Beyond the hamlet, by the little church, you meet the Genga/Rocchetta road

again (**1h40min**). Follow this uphill
again for just under 500m, to a
right-hand bend, from where the
twin towers of Rochetta's church
come into view. At this point — in
front of a stand of reeds — climb
(pathless) steeply up to the left along
the edge of a field and across an
overgrown meadow. After 100m
you come to a small road, which you
follow to the left for another 100m,
between the few houses of **Rocchetta Alta** (**1h55min**).

At the end of the surfaced road
continue on the grassy trail,
climbing a little to the right. Five
minutes from Rocchetta Alta the
trail divides: take the left-hand, less
steep fork, uphill (occasional red and
white waymarks of Route 142). The
trail veers right, gently climbing.
Ten minutes from Rocchetta Alta
you have a first view over undulating
wooded mountains. A little later, at
the foot of a steep eroded slope with
reddish rock (**2h10min**), the trail
narrows to a path and climbs more
steeply, first through blackberry
bushes and then through a shady
wood. Having curved to the right,
you reach another **superb viewpoint**
(**2h20min**) with a long view
towards the successive ranges of the
Apennines. The path rises almost
imperceptibly along the southern
flanks of Monte Ameno, studded
with cypresses, then turns a little to
the left and descends gently south. A
badly-eroded small scree (20m
across) requires care on this section.
The lovely path descends steadily
and offers views into the remote
wooded surroundings. After a
distinct bend to the left through an
oak wood, you reach a clearing
where the path widens to a grassy
trail. This descends south, now
through pine trees. Veering left, you
come back to the junction and your
outgoing route (**2h55min**).
Retrace your steps for some 20
minutes, back to **Monticelli**
(**3h15min**).

*Near Trivio (top) and limestone cliffs
above Valle Scappuccia*

Walk 24: THE GOLA DELLA ROSSA NEAR FRASASSI

Distance/time: 16km; just under 5h
Grade: quite strenuous, with an overall ascent/descent of 750m; easy orientation (the route is signposted)
Equipment: as pages 46-47
Refreshments: none en route
How to get there: 🚌 from San Vittore Terme via Pierosara (Car tour 6 at the 137km-point) to the junction in front of the first houses of Cerqueto; no public transport
Shorter walk 1: 10km; 3h05min; moderate, with an overall ascent/descent of 500m: omit the diversion to Monte Murano.
Shorter walk 2: 30min less than the main walk, but *difficult (on a very exposed path initially; you must be sure-footed, with a head for heights).* At the

junction 50m before the **Grotta del Vernino** (just before the 1h55min-point) fork left, to follow a narrow path rising steeply along the gravel slope (red and white waymarks, ⌐: Monte Murano 107b). After 10 minutes of very steep zig-zags the path veers right (southeast), then runs less steeply along the sheer hill-side of Monte Tordina. Curving to the left round a rocky promontory with views down to the Esino Valley, you come to an easier path. With little ascent, this takes you along the southeastern slopes of Monte Tordina and Monte Foglia, with fine long views. At the grassy **saddle below Monte Murano** pick up the main walk again, at the 3h10min-point.

The creation of the Frasassi Nature Reserve has not prevented the construction of an expressway and the continued existence of a large quarry within the protected area. Nevertheless some pleasant walks through unspoilt countryside still exist around the gorges of the Esino and Sentino rivers, lined by steep limestone cliffs. This walk leads initially into the remote Valle del Vernino, with its varied vegetation and a cave leading deep into Monte Tordina. Afterwards we climb Monte Murano for a good view over the mountainous surroundings.

Starting point is the junction in front of the group of houses 300m north of **Cerqueto**. Follow the surfaced side-road branching off furthest to the right from the main road down to Genga. Within five minutes you come to **Cerqueto**. At the edge of this partly-deserted hamlet, by the public wash-house, take the left (upper) lane and leave Cerqueto on an earthen track (⌐: Sentiero Cerqueto–Palombara). Some 150m beyond the hamlet, where the track starts to rise, follow the signs, to fork right on a path. This descends gently with some zigzags through a conifer wood, passes a spring, and comes to a refuge (**Rifugio**) with benches and a table. From here you have a nice view towards wooded slopes where pencil-thin cypresses grow in

profusion. Behind the building the path continues over stony terrain straight on along the hillside, then veers right, to zigzag down more steeply through the conifer wood. Finally a stony, somewhat tricky path takes you down to a small road. Turning left alongside a railway line and the valley's main road, this takes you past the few houses of **Palombara** to a place for a break, at the foot of a steep cliff with a shrine (**45min**).
In front of the railway level crossing take the old road to the left, to walk into the **valley of the river Esino**, framed by steep rocks. At a junction, go left, to cross the new expressway on a bridge. Five minutes later you come to a barrier fence (**55min**), from where the use of the old road is forbidden — even for walkers.

In the Esino Valley

will hear is birdsong. At the following Y-fork, go right (↑: Grotta del Vernino). A short way further on, a sign fixed to a barrier tells you that because of nesting bats, the Vernino Cave may not be entered between 15 November and 15 March. Behind the barrier the trail narrows to a pleasant path lined by holm oaks and cypresses. At the next junction (**1h15min**), turn right again (east) on a grassy path. (After a few paces, a path branching off sharp left would take you 50m to a stone hut in a meadow — another pleasant place for a break.) The path straight ahead climbs towards the **limestone cliffs of Monte Tordina**, after five minutes veering to the left, to continue in a northerly direction again. You steadily gain height in the shade of the rock face of Monte

Around 30m in front of the barrier, turn left uphill on a trail (↑: Grotta del Vernino/Monte Murano, Route 107a). This leads north into the remote **Valle del Vernino** where, instead of traffic, the only sound you

Tordina, which rises above on the right. Beyond a wooded section and a zigzag, you reach another signposted junction (**1h40min**) but, before continuing straight ahead on Route 107a, turn right for a **diversion** to the Vernino Cave (⌐: Grotta del Vernino, Route 107b).

The small path zigzags up the wooded slopes in a northeasterly direction. After 10 minutes, beyond a right-hand bend, you reach a junction at the bottom of a gravel slope, where Route 107b rises steeply to the left *(Shorter walk 2)*. Continuing 50m straight ahead, you stand in front of the **Grotta del Vernino** (**1h55min**). If you believe Italian guide books, it is possible (equipped with a good torch) to walk for several hundred metres inside this cave without major problems. I didn't try it. If you do, be very careful!)

Retracing your steps, return to the junction 10 minutes below the Vernino Cave (**2h05min**), from where you again follow Route 107a (⌐: Valico Colle di Cupi). Somewhat overgrown, this path leads in three minutes to a small drystone ruin, which you pass on your right. Walk another 10m, to the edge of the hill. Turning right from here, the faint path ascends a gravel slope for 50m, then becomes clearer and less overgrown as it rises northwest. With far-reaching views over the Vernino Valley, the path leads through a drystone wall, then makes another zigzag. At the upper end of the Vernino Valley the route veers to the left and crosses a stream bed (**2h20min**). Now rising to the south, you pass the left turning of Route 107c and come onto a small plain with abundant gorse and rose hips. Following a flat trail 200m to the west, you meet a track at the saddle **Valico Colle di Cupi** (**2h30min**).

To climb Monte Murano, follow this to the right uphill (⌐: 107AG Monte Murano). After a stony stretch, the track is good under foot; it runs through a wood to a small road (**2h55min**). Go right uphill (⌐: 143 Monte Murano), to a pass in a conifer wood. The road then passes the Casa della Parrocchia and veers left round the slopes of Monte Foglia with far-reaching views. The sealed road ends at a large transmitter mast. The ongoing route descends straight ahead into a **grassy saddle** at the foot of Monte Murano (**3h10min**). In early summer yellow-blooming broom grows here in abundance.

Turn right on a trail, climbing Monte Murano. You go through a little wood, then rise diagonally left to an iron cross. From here a path to the right takes you to the **summit of Monte Murano** (882m; **3h30min**), with panoramic views.

Back at the **grassy saddle**, follow a trail straight ahead for 100m, to the restored **Case Marcellini**. Behind the building you pass a pond and continue straight on along a gently-climbing path along the grassy northern hillside of Monte Foglia, enjoying long views to the northeast. Keep to the left of a line of bushes, climb through some dark conifers (keeping a little to the left), and come back to the small surfaced road. Retracing your steps, you walk back to the pass of **Vallico Colle di Cupi** (**4h15min**).

From here continue straight ahead on the main track (⌐: Cerqueto Route 107AG). Turn left at the Y-fork three minutes later, to rise again a short way. The track then runs along the southeastern hillside of Monte San Pietro with good views. Always keep to the main route; after 10 more minutes this veers to the right (north) and comes to a T-junction by a barrier. Heading down to the left, you return to the starting point 300m north of **Cerqueto** (**4h50min**).

Walk 25: THROUGH THE APENNINES NEAR FABRIANO

See photograph page 34
Distance/time: 15km; 4h45min
Grade: fairly strenuous, with an overall ascent/descent of about 650m. The last half hour of the path to San Cataldo is a little overgrown and not always clear, otherwise navigation is easy despite the lack of waymarks
Equipment: as pages 46-47; take sufficient drinking water
Refreshments: none en route
How to get there: 🚗 to Esanatoglia (Car tour 6 at the 216km-point); 🚌 on working days 10 buses a day from Fabriano and Matelica to Esanatoglia
Longer variation: 18km; 5h45min; strenuous, with 850m of ascent/descent. Follow the main walk past the wood (1h45min), then keep to the main track, which veers right

(north) and rises along the eastern flanks of Monte Giuoco del Pallone. The trail narrows, crosses the edge of a wood and leads onto the meadows of **Monte Antensa** (1228m). Following the summit ridge south you come to neighbouring **Monte Giuoco del Pallone** (1227m; cairn, trig point). Keeping a little to the eastern side of the ridge, follow a faint path over rocky ground to descend to the lowest point on the ridge (1090m), then pick up the main walk at the 2h15min-point.
Short walk: 7km; 2h15min; easy, with 250m ascent/descent. At the 1h-point in the main walk turn right. Follow the main walk from the 3h25min-point, to return to Esanatoglia via San Cataldo.

The little hermitage church of San Cataldo, our last goal on this walk, perches like an eagle's nest on the steep rocky slopes above Esanatoglia. Before reaching this we explore the remote mountains around Monte Giuoco del Pallone, one of the many unknown summits of the central Apennines around Fabriano. The landscape en route is very typical for this rarely-visited area: pines, holm oaks, gorse and juniper grow on the stony lower slopes exposed to the sun, while higher up we rise through deciduous woods with beeches and oaks to grassy summit ridges with vast panoramas. Only rarely will you see a human being up here; more likely you will meet groups of horses roaming freely.

Starting out at the entrance to the *centro storico* in the small town of **Esanatoglia**, go through a gate into Piazza Cavour and continue via a second gate onto Corso V Emanuele II. This takes you through the old town, climbing across the town hall square and leaves the old town by a third gate. Turn left on a small road, past the ruins of an old paper mill and the last houses of Esanatoglia, emerging in the green Esino Valley. Around 250m beyond the edge of the village (50m past a trail off left to a concrete shed), fork right on a stony old mule path (🏳: San Cataldo/Case Quagna, red/white waymarks). It rises steadily south-

west along the hillside above the Esino Valley. After climbing for 10 minutes, ignore the smaller path off right for 'Tornanti'. To the north, high on a rock, the small church of San Cataldo comes into view. After a patch of wood the path comes to another fork with wooden signposts, where the San Cataldo route goes right (735m, **1h**). *(We will use this route later to return to Esanatoglia; for now, the Short walk turns right at this junction.)*
Keep to the main path straight ahead, again rising through woods (red/white waymarks of Route 141).In 10 minutes you meet a track. Follow it 100m downhill.

Then, by a small ruin on the left, turn right on a well-worn path (*no waymarks*). This climbs through juniper, with far-reaching views, back to the track. Follow the track uphill for 10 minutes, then fork right on a faint path, to rise 30m to a parallel trail running along a low shoulder.

You reach the main track for a third time at the foot of barren Monte Giuoco del Pallone, a long north-south running ridge. A few paces ahead, this divides (**1h35min**). Go right, to follow a white gravel track through a small wood. Emerging from the wood, continue a little to the left along a grassy trail (**1h45min**). *(But for the Longer variation, keep right, north, on the main track.)* The trail climbs the grassy slopes straight ahead, to a **flat saddle** (1090m; **2h15min**) between Monte Giuoco del Pallone (1227m) and the low elevation of Pizzinetto di Mutola (1125m). This is a good viewpoint west across the valley of Campodonico to the main ridge of the Umbrian Apennines.

From here follow the treeless summit ridge south for 10 minutes, enjoying long views over the remote mountain area. Circling to the left, you pass the knoll of **Pizzinetto di Mutola** and reach the beginning of a pale gravel path. This descends along the northeastern hillside, back to the 1h40min-point of the outgoing route (**2h50min**). Go right, back through the small wood. Follow the main track a good 15 minutes; then, in the right-hand bend, go straight ahead on your outgoing path for five minutes, back to the **fork with signposts at the 1h-point** in the main walk (**3h25min**).

Fork left (▪: San Cataldo/Fonte dell'Olmo, red/white waymarks of Route 141). The path rises gently in the shade of the woods. After about 10 minutes it passes a small spring on the left and a clearing on the right, before becoming steeper for a short stretch and then contouring the southeastern flanks of Monte Corsegno with its limestone cliffs. Eventually you descend a short way to the **Eremo San Cataldo** (766m; **4h10min**).

From the hermitage follow the Stations of the Cross down to a wide track. Fork right on a short-cut path with yellow markings (▪: La Corta). Descending steeply through woods, it crosses the wide track, veers right, and rejoins the (now tarred) track at the **Convento Capuccini**. Ignore further (steep) short-cuts; follow the road some 30m past the gate, then turn right downhill on a track. With views down onto the tiled roofs of destination, this takes you back to the starting point in **Esanatoglia** in 15 minutes (**4h45min**).

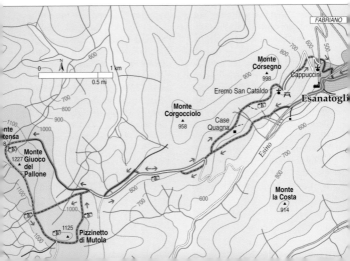

Walk 26: HERMITS' CAVES ABOVE THE FIASTRONE GORGE

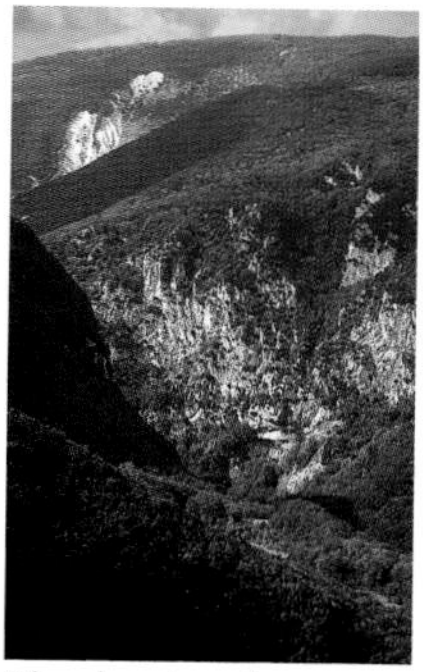

View down into the Fiastrone Gorge

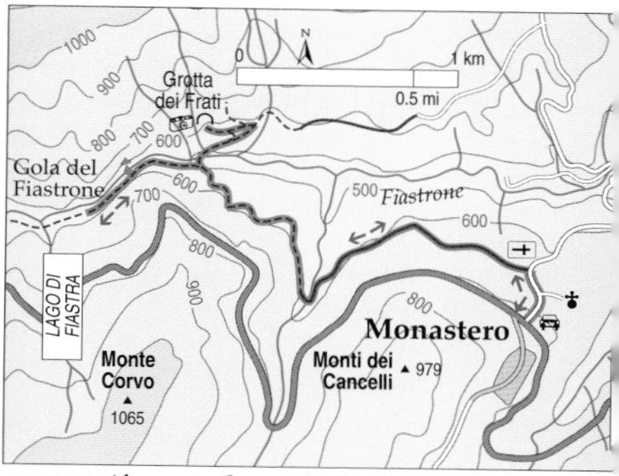

Distance/time: 9km; 3h30min

Grade: moderate, with an ascent/descent of 400m

Equipment: as pages 46-47; plastic sandals an asset when there is a lot of water in the gorge

Refreshments: none en route

How to get there: 🚗 to Monastero (Car tour 8 at the 106km-point); no public transport

A little-known but very impressive gorge criss-crosses the rocky ground on the northern side of the Sibillini Mountains below Lake Fiastra. Only from the very bottom of the valley can you see the sheer, narrow cliffs of the Gola del Fiastrone. After dry periods it is possible to walk quite a way upstream into this dark ravine. After strong rains small waterfalls pour down from the cliffs, the stream runs high, and you'll probably have to return after a short stretch. Hidden in the rocks on the slopes above lie the caves of the Grotta dei Frati, where a group of medieval monks retreated for meditation — a typical remote natural site in the spirit of the early Franciscans.

Start the walk at the edge of **Monastero**. Coming from the east, descend a track to the right (50m before the turning left up to Monastero village; ⚑: Grotta dei Frati/Valle del Fiastrone). This track leads past a little abbey on your right, to the **cemetery**. Turn left on a track in front of the cemetery walls; after five minutes it starts descending in a westerly direction. The track bends sharp right and crosses a stream bed (**25min**; some red arrows as waymarks), after which it narrows to a shady path. After a clearing with a meadow (**35min**) you zigzag down more steeply through the wood. At a junction just above the bottom of the valley (**50min**), go left. The path now runs alongside the Fiastrone stream, leading west into the narrowing valley. Having followed the watercourse for around 15 minutes, your path disappears into a cleft of high reddish cliffs, soon passing underneath a rocky arch (**1h15min**). You are now in the **Gola del Fiastrone**; how far you can explore upstream depends on the amount of water in the streambed. From the cleft retrace your steps for 10 minutes along the right bank of the stream. When you see a red waymark on a tree stump and a little signpost 'Grotta dei Frati' on your left, cross the Fiastrone and rise steeply up the far bank for several metres, to a path. Follow this to the right uphill, through the woods. At the next junction it is best *not* to take the left-hand, waymarked path (too steep), but keep right. At the next junction, turn sharp left (**1h45min**; ▐: Grotta). You gain height along the slopes north of the Fiastrone Valley. At the next, Y-fork, where

the path to the right would lead further uphill to Monte Fiegni, go left. In five minutes you reach the **Grotta dei Frati** (**2h05min**) high above the gorge at the foot of limestone cliffs. Inside the caves the hermits have built a little chapel, with a touching crib nearby. From here retrace your outgoing route back to starting point at the edge of **Monastero** (**3h30min**).

Walk 27: Around Monte delle Rose

Walk 27: ABOVE THE CASTELLUCCIO PLATEAU

See also photos on pages 4-5, 112 and the cover	Refreshments: none en route
Distance/time: 14km; 4h15min	How to get there: 🚗 to Castelluccio (Car tour 5 at the 134km-point, Car tour 8 at the 166km-point); 🚌 bus between Norcia and Castelluccio on *Thursdays only*
Grade: moderate, with an overall ascent/descent of 600m; waymarks are rare, but orientation is easy	
Equipment: as pages 46-47; also plenty of drinking water, sunhat	Walking map: Monti Sibillini, Carta dei Sentieri, CAI, 1:25,000

It's not only the name Altopiano di Castelluccio that is reminiscent of the high plains of South America: a vast grassy plain, framed by barren mountains, stretches before us. Only one little village lies up here in splendid isolation. The bleak landscape around the dried-up glacial lake is in some respects the result of human activity. The original beech forests have been decimated by extensive tree-felling. Some remains of the once-large woodlands can be found in Valle Canetra at the start of the walk, from where we climb the panoramic mountains to the west of the high plateau. This landscape is especially beautiful in early summer, when wild flowers in bloom carpet the ground. Autumn brings intense colours, too, when the strong russet foliage of the beeches contrasts with the pale yellow grassland and the high mountain ridges, powdered by the first snowfalls, stand out brightly against a deep blue sky.

Leave **Castelluccio** to the north, following the road to Visso for 150m. Then turn left on the track to nearby Agriturismo la Valle delle Aquile. Initially it runs parallel to the road, then veers left, to descend into the remote **Valle Canetra**, where many peonies are in blossom at the end of May. After a good 20 minutes' walk from Castelluccio the track describes an S-curve and passes a drinking-trough for cattle at the **Fonte Valle Canetra** (**30min**). Here the track narrows to a grassy trail, which gently climbs along the bottom of the valley, with the forest on the left and the bleak slopes of Monte Lieto on the right. Some 30 minutes from the spring the trail veers left (southwest), passes 50m to the right of a blue EU-signboard and enters a thin beech wood, becoming steep and stony. Watch for a cairn 15 minutes above the EU signboard and turn right on a small stony trail (**1h20min**). The trail swings left, then right, to

pass through another patch of beech wood. Then take the path rising steeply across grassy slopes, with far-off views down into Valle Canetra. It heads north towards the lowest point of the ridge connecting Monte Lieto and Monte delle Rose. Climb — pathless — for the last 100m to the **saddle** (1687m; **1h45min**). On the far side of the saddle take the undulating trail which contours the steep and rocky northern slopes of Monte delle Rose. Some 10 minutes from the saddle this veers right, to climb to the **grassy pass** between Monte Fausole and Monte delle Rose (1701m; **2h10min**). Turn sharp left here, *on no proper path,* to rise steeply for around 15 minutes along a sloping meadow. At the end of the ascent you come to the start of a clear trail. Before continuing straight on, take a diversion to the right, by climbing 50m in height onto the barren summit of **Monte delle Rose** (1864m; **2h35min**), a pleasant viewpoint.

Castelluccio village (top) and another view of the plain (left; see also pages 4-5)

3000ft metres below you, the dark walls and towers of Norcia rise out of the haze. The clear path passes to the right of a knoll (1800m), beyond which you reach a junction **high above the plain of the Piano Grande (3h10min).**

Take the path to the left; within five minutes you reach a track coming from the foot of a rounded hill, Poggio di Croce (1833m). Descend this easily followed track for just under an hour, enjoying far-reaching views out across the superb high plain of the Piano Grande, back to **Castelluccio (4h15min).**

Then retrace your steps to the trail and follow it southeast — a lovely panoramic route along the eastern hillside of Monte delle Rose. Gently descending, you come to a large grassy ridge. On the right, 1000m/

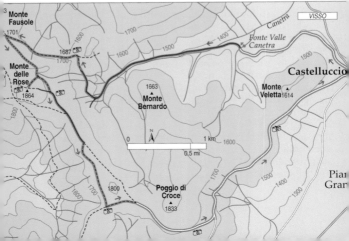

Walk 28: ALONG THE SLOPES OF MONTE UTERO

Distance/time: 14km; 4h
Grade: moderate, with an overall ascent/descent of 550m
Equipment: as pages 46-47
Refreshments: none en route
How to get there: 🚗 see Car tour 5 at the 125km-point. From the pass of **Forca Canapine** (1541m), where the road from Norcia makes a sharp

left-hand bend, take the wide track leading uphill to the south. Follow this for just under 1km to the starting point, the little refuge **Rifugio La Stalla** (also called Rifugio Regoli; 1574m) on the right, where you can park. No public transport

To the south of the Monti Sibillini, the ridge between Umbria and Lazio (Latium) offers more good hiking possibilities. This is a landscape of unlimited views: a high sky arches above the nearly- treeless, far-reaching grassy summits; in the distance the steep ridges of Abruzzi become blurred in the haze; and groups of half-wild horses roam around large meadows to ponds where they can slake their thirst. From the rounded summit of Monte Utero (1807m), the highest point of this walk, you have a wide panoramic view over the mountains in the heart of Italy, where the Monti Sibillini (2476m), Monti della Laga (2458m), Gran Sasso (2912m) and Monte Terminillo (2216m) are the most prominent ranges.

Start out behind **Rifugio La Stalla**: either follow the main track straight ahead or the path running alongside it on the left. Both climb steeply for 150m, then lead into an open landscape of grassy slopes. After around 30 minutes from the refuge, a depression with some tiny lakes comes into view below on the left. Herds of cattle and groups of half-wild horses gather at these ponds, which almost dry up in high summer. Ignoring trails turning off to the left, keep straight ahead (north), to rise 50m in height, to the saddle of **Forca dei Copelli** (1626m; **50 min.**) east of Monte dei Signori (1781m). From here take a grassy trail a little to the right and climb to the edge of a beech wood. Walk up through the beeches to the **saddle** south of Monte dei Signori (1708m; **1h05min**).
Here you ignore the trail to the right (you will come back on it later). Instead, walk uphill south along the grassy slopes on no clear path, to rise onto a nameless **elevation at 1769m** (**1h20min**), with a vast

panoramic view. From here follow a path to the south, which descends a short way along the ridge leading towards Monte Utero. A good 10 minutes from elevation 1769m the path crosses a small clearing with a meadow, then ascends steeply along the left hillside, initially through the woods and then along a grassy slope. At the end of the climb you step onto the flat panoramic summit of **Monte Utero** (1807m; **1h45min**).
Keeping to the ridge, walk downhill five minutes, to the edge of a little wood, which you cross alongside a long narrow clearing. From the end of the clearing take a descending trail straight onto a **meadow on a saddle** (1661m, **2h**). Circle to the right on the main trail, to descend northwest across slopes covered by large pastures, with views down into the valley of Norcia. The trail becomes clearer and veers far right to the edge of the woods, where it turns sharply to the left, down to a T-junction at the troughs of the **Fonte d'Utero** spring (1568m, **2h15min**).

At the Forca dei Copelli (top) and the ponds below the pass, where cattle and half-wild horses slake their thirst

Turn sharp right on a track here, initially going uphill a short way. It then contours along the western hillside of Monte Utero, passing a familiar-looking beech wood. Some 15 minutes from Fonte d'Utero the track rises to a barren shoulder (**2h45min**). At the junction, where the main track starts descending straight ahead towards the edge of the wood, turn right on a trail, heading east. You climb steeply for 10 minutes, then the trail flattens out, crosses a stand of beeches and 116

veers to the left. Following a grassy ridge, you come back to the **saddle at 1708m** (**3h**).

Retracing your steps, return to the **Rifugio La Stalla** (**4h**).

Walk 29: FROM CASTELLUCCIO TO LAGO DI PILATO

Distance/time: 11km; 4h30min
Grade: quite strenuous out-and-back mountain walking; overall ascent/descent of around 550m
Equipment: as pages 46-47
Refreshments: none en route
How to get there: 🚌 see Car tour 5 at the 134km point or Car tour 8 at the 166km-point. Approaching Castelluccio from the south, turn right on a wide track 200m before the

sharp left-hand bend below the village hill. At the next junction take the main fork a little to the left, which leads northeast through a bleak valley to a shepherds' hut, **Capanna Ghezzi** (1570m), where you can park. No public transport
Note: An endangered species of tiny crayfish lives in Lake Pilato; *it is absolutely forbidden to walk on the shore or throw stones into the water.*

The massive ridge of Monte Argentella (2200m) and Cima del Redentore (2448m, the highest mountain in Umbria), rises steeply from the corn and lentil fields on the vast plains to the east of Castelluccio. Hidden behind the ridge lies little Lago di Pilato, a blue spot of water at the foot of the vertical cliffs of Pizzo del Diavolo (Devil's Peak). Numerous legends surround this remote and beautiful Alpine setting high in the mountains. Pontius Pilate is said to be drowned in the lake; other tales say that Satan plies his evil trade up here. Science only acknowledges one inhabitant: the Chirocefalo del Marchesoni, a tiny sweetwater crayfish, which is unique to Lago di Pilato.

Start out at **Capanna Ghezzi**, between the building and a drinking trough: walk 50m up the grassy slope, then turn right on a path. This veers to the right, becomes clearer, and climbs the flat shoulder to the southeast of the shepherds' hut. Here you cross the **meadows of Pianacce**, where the path runs north

for around 10 minutes. At the following junction, where CAI Route 5 continues straight ahead towards Monte Porche (2273m), take Route 2 to the right. Along this well-worn path traversing the southern hillside, you enjoy superb views down onto the Castelluccio Plateau. At the end of the ascent you

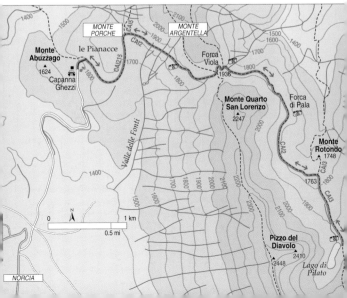

Two faces of Lago di Pilato

On the far side of the saddle the path zigzags steeply downhill for around five minutes, then veers right, to undulate along the northeastern slopes of Monte Quarto San Lorenzo. On the left, far below, the valley of Foce comes into view. The path now leads through Alpine scenery into the valley below Monte Vettore (2476m). Beyond the saddle of **Forca di Pala** (1852m) you have to cross a boulder field, where snow sometimes lingers into July. Curving left, you descend all the way down to the valley floor (1763m), where you meet CAI Route 3 coming up from Foce (**1h50min**).

From here it's a steep climb, with the sheer rockface of Pizzo del Diavolo rising in northwest above the path. Finally the blue and brightly-shining surface of **Lago di Pilato** comes into view (1940m; **2h30min**). In dry summers the lake — at most 7m deep — shrinks to two little ponds connected by a small stretch of water.

From the lake retrace your steps to the **Capanne Ghezzi** (**4h30min**).

come to the **Forca Viola** (1936m; **1h05min**), a grassy pass between Monte Argentella (2200m) and Monte Quarto San Lorenzo (2247m).

Walk 30: BELOW THE ROCKY PYRAMID OF MONTE BOVE

7Photograph on page 43
Distance/time: 14km; 4h40min
Grade: strenuous, with an overall
ascent/descent of around 800m; easy
navigation; mainly on good tracks,
trails and mountain paths
Equipment: as pages 46-47. Don't
forget rain protection even on fine
days; in these high mountains the
weather can change quickly.
Refreshments: none en route; the
Rifugio del Fargno is seldom open
How to get there: 🚌 to Casali, 9km
northeast of Visso (the 142km-point
on Car tour 8); no public transport
Variation 1 (+110m ascent/
15min): At the junction 30m before
the boundary stone at the 2h25min-
point, fork right. Follow a steep path
northeast, to the pass of **Forca Angagnola** (1924m; long view to the
east down into the Ambro Valley).
From the saddle take a path left

along the western hillside of Pizzo
Tre Vescovi. Gently descending, you
reach the pass of Forca del Fargno in
20 minutes. Pick up the main walk
again at the 3h-point.
**Variation 2: across Pizzo Tre
Vescovi** (+280m ascent/45min):
Do Variation 1, but from **Forca
Angagnola** keep to the partly-rocky
ridge, which climbs northeast onto
the flat summit viewpoint of **Pizzo
Tre Vescovi** (2092m). Around 50m
before the cross on top, take a faint
path that starts on the right and
descends along the northeastern
slopes towards Monte Acuto
(2035m). At the saddle below
Monte Acuto turn left on a well-
trodden path, descending the
northern slopes of Pizzo Tre Vescovi
down to pass of Forca del Fargno.
Pick up the main walk again at the
3h-point.

M onte Bove is probably the most impressive mountain in the
entire Sibillini range. Like an Alpine limestone peak, its
sheer, mighty northern rockface looms above the Ussita torrent.
This walk leads in the shade of its high cliffs through the remote
Val di Panico up to the grassy slopes of Pizzo Tre Vescovi, from
where we enjoy superb views. Because of the height gain the walk
is quite strenuous, but nowhere along the route are mountaineering skills required.

Starting point is the small Romanesque church of **Casali** (1080m) at
the end of the surfaced road coming
up from Ussita. Continue straight
on past the church along the wide
track leading into the Ussita Valley.
After 100m turn left uphill on a
narrower track. After a short way
this veers right, passes a cross, runs
over a stream bed and climbs more
steeply to the right. Ascending
through a beech wood you come to
another track (**15min**). Again go
right, now gently descending with
views to the rock face of Monte
Bove Nord (2112m). When you
rejoin the main track coming up
from Casali (**25min**), follow it
further into the valley. Mighty
Monte Bove Nord rises to the south

above the ravine of the Ussita
torrent, while the steep rock-strewn
sloping meadows of Monte
Rotondo (2102m) and Pizzo Tre
Vescovi (2092m) border the valley
to the east. The track curves more
and more to the south until, at the
end of the valley, it makes a
distinct **bend to the right** (1346m;
50min).
At the beginning of the bend take a
path leading straight off the track,
going uphill into the **Valle di
Panico**. After about five minutes
follow a trail to the right, to the edge
of the woods. At this point, in front
of a little concrete building (spring),
turn left uphill on a steep gravel
path. This leads within 10 minutes
to a sloping meadow, which you

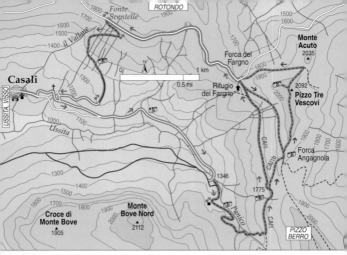

skirt to the left — at the right of the valley. At the end of the meadow climb sharply to the right, to the edge of a beech wood backed by steep limestone cliffs. Turn left before the woods, to return to the bottom of Valle di Panico. Then continue rising up the valley until you come to a rocky **promontory** protruding north into the valley (**1h45min**).

Turn left in front of the promontory and follow a small, sometimes-faint path, climbing more steeply to the east. After about 15 minutes you meet a clearer path running along the western hillside. Turn left and follow this north (occasional red and white waymarks of CAI Route 1). This climbs a short way, then crosses a promontory with a meadow, a nice spot for a break. With good views across Valle di Panico towards Monte Bove, continue along a narrow but good path traversing the open hillside. Curving right, the path comes to a Y-fork 20m in front of a sloping gully (1775m; **2h25min**); go left, after 30m passing an **old boundary stone** 10m above on the right. (*The Variations go right here.*) A flat narrow path takes you along the grassy slopes on the western slopes of the long ridge between Pizzo Berro and Pizzo Tre Vescovi. A good 20 minutes from the

120

boundary stone, the path divides again: take the faint fork to the right of the meadows, climbing again for a short time. The trail becomes more distinct and takes you to a bunker-like **refuge** 50m south of **Forca del Fargno** (**3h**).

Beyond the building join the wide track crossing this pass. Follow the main route northwest along the slopes of barren Monte Rotondo, high above Ussita Valley. Some 20 minutes from the refuge you pass a reddish-coloured eroded slope on the right and, 10 minutes later, reach a spring, **Fonte Scentelle**, where horses sometimes graze (**3h35min**). Take the grassy trail forking off sharp left just *before* this spring. Follow it 300m southeast downhill, past some young conifers, to a watering place for cattle (old bath tubs). In front of the tubs turn sharp right on a gravel path. This crosses a badly-eroded slope and soon veers left (south). With constant views towards Monte Bove, descend fairly gently on a clear trail. Beyond a short stretch through some pastures and past a **spring** (**4h20min**), turn right downhill on a track. At the junction 10 minutes later, go sharp left on a forest track. In three minutes you meet your outgoing track; turn right downhill and retrace your steps back to **Casali** (**4h40min**).

Walk 31: MOUNTAIN TRAILS ABOVE THE AMBRO VALLEY

Distance/time: 20km; 6h15min
Grade: a demanding walk for experienced hikers, with 900m ascent/descent. A good sense for orientation is needed, and you must be surefooted. Do *not* walk alone.
Equipment: as pages 46-47; also ample food and drinking water
Refreshments: none en route; bars and restaurant at the starting point
How to get there: 🚌 to Madonna dell'Ambro; the access road is 5km south of Amandola (the 81km-point on Car tour 8); no public transport
Variation: 19km; 5h15min; grade as main walk (800m ascent/descent). An out-and-back route, starting from Fonte Vecchia, west of Vetice village. Access by 🚌: 3km west of Montefortino, turn left from the main valley road to Madonna dell'Ambro and take a side road uphill to Vetice. Beyond the first houses turn sharp right and pass the upper group of houses of Vetice. From here follow a wide bumpy track 2km west

uphill, to a junction in front of the troughs of **Fonte Vecchia** (parking possible 50m uphill to the left).
Start out in front of **Fonte Vecchia**: turn right on a track which gently climbs northwest through the meadows and fields of Campi di Vetice. The reddish-hued rock pyramid of Balzo Rosso (1444m) rises straight in front of you on the far side of the valley. At the end of the initial ascent the track passes the concrete troughs of another drinking water source (**15min**), then descends for around 5min. After this two trails join from the right in quick succession (**25min**). The second is the main walk route coming up from Madonna dell'Ambro. Follow the main walk from the 35min-point to the **source of the Ambro** (**3h**), then retrace your steps to **Fonte Vecchia** (**5h15min**).
Walking map: Monti Sibillini, Carta dei Sentieri, Club Alpino Italiano, 1:25,000

This long walk, one of the most demanding but most beautiful in this book, leads deep into the remote Monti Sibillini. We follow small trails and paths traversing the hillsides high above the ravine of the Ambro Stream, which we circle in its entirety. The route runs through shady beech woods and across open meadows and pastures with far-reaching views towards the dramatic mountain landscape at the foot of Monte Priora (2332m). There is not a single inhabited house en route, and only seldom will you meet another hiker. For hours you walk alone through untouched nature, far away from modern civilisation.

Starting point is the sanctuary of **Madonna dell'Ambro**. Opposite the church, cross the Ambro Stream on a footbridge. Then go straight uphill through pines for 100m before veering right on a path (red and white; also orange waymarks). This rises steeply in tight zigzags, initially as a sunken forest path. Beyond a stretch of nearly flat walking in a westerly direction, the path veers left, to gain more height. You come to a forest trail, which you follow to the left for 200m, to a

forest track. Turn sharp right here *(no waymarks)*. Circling to the left, the track climbs through a thin beech wood, crosses another forest track, and rises in a southeasterly direction to a **wider track** (**35min**). *(The Variation starting from Fonte Vecchia joins here.)*
Follow this track to the right. The track ascends, describes a S-curve and leads back into a thick beech wood, through which it climbs steadily (occasional faded red and white waymarks). The track narrows

121

Above: near Fonte Vecchia; below: the Ambro Valley near the spring

to a path (**1h**) and, 10 minutes later, below the steep cliffs of Monte Pizzo, it zigzags uphill along the open hillside offering a long view to the east. Around 5 minutes later the path flattens out and runs along the slopes high above the Ambro Valley. It's a lovely path running alongside small meadows and through snatches of woods, eventually veering right, across the **pastures of Prato Porfidia**. Only the ruins of some stone huts remain from this shepherds' settlement. Five minutes past here, a **grassy promontory** on the right gives you a pleasant view down into Ambro Gorge (1237m; **1h40min**).

The path leads from here back into

the beech woods. Some 10 minutes from the viewpoint you cross a first eroded slope (1190m). Going uphill again you come 20 minutes later to a second eroded area with fallen trees across the route, which you have circumvent by taking a faint path higher up. Then the path climbs steeply for 15 more minutes, to a **saddle/promontory** at the foot of an as yet unseen massive limestone rock (1430m; **2h30min**).

Around three minutes later you leave the woods. The path descends a bit, veers right and crosses a sloping stream bed. The steep rock-strewn slopes of Monte Priora (2332m) tower up in the south. The path then leads back into the woods and divides (**2h55min**): go right, gently descending in a westerly direction, down towards the Ambro Valley. Becoming a little overgrown, the path then leads through some bushes towards a flat stream bed. Before this gully, take a path 50m down to the right, to where the overgrown **Sorgente dell'Ambro** (source) rises from a little cave (1245m; **3h10min**).

Here you cross the stream and follow a narrow grassy path northeast up the opposite slope. In five minutes you join another path and head right. After 20m the path circles to the left round a promontory (stabilised by an iron grating), and descends to the edge of the woods (occasional faded blue and red waymarks). Beyond the wood ascend a steep narrow path across a sloping meadow, to a pass west of

the hilltop called **Le Roccacce**, strewn with rock rubble (1336m; **3h35min**).

Beyond the pass head straight down through the woods for 100m. Turning right, the path then descends beside some rocks to a sloping meadow offering a long view to the east. From here the stony path descends back into woods, where it meets the start of a trail: keep straight on. This pleasant, easy trail continues eastwards above the Ambro Valley, sometimes in the shade of high beeches, sometimes crossing open meadows with views into remote mountain scenery.

Beyond a **clearing by a ruin** (**4h15min**) the trail rises a little once more. Now silver firs and larches also grow beside the route. Descending once more, you finally reach the spring of **Fonte Faggi** by the **Rifugio San Giovanni Gualberto** (**4h50min**).

Turn right about 30m in front of the refuge, to follow a path downhill through undergrowth. After 100m this veers left to the edge of the woods, where it becomes clearer. Around 20 minutes from the refuge the path circles to the left around the hillside and opens up a view towards abrupt high cliffs. The next 10 minutes sees some slightly tricky walking on a stony path. Go left at a junction, skirting the foot of **Balzo Rosso**, a vertical reddish rock face looming above the path. After 200m (50m past a stone trough), turn sharp right on a forest trail (**5h35min**). Follow this downhill towards the Ambro Valley for a good 15 minutes. At a right-hand bend take a path branching off to the left. A good five minutes later you cross an eroded slope (secured by a rope), and descend to a spring (**6h**). Then take the trail down to the left (through a badly-eroded, skiddy area, where you should *keep back from the steep drop!*), to return to **Madonna dell'Ambro** (**6h15min**).

Walk 32: THROUGH THE INFERNACCIO GORGE

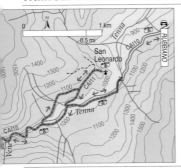

Distance/time: 9km; 3h
Grade: quite easy, despite the wild scenery, with a total ascent/descent of around 400m; easy orientation
Equipment: as pages 46-47
Refreshments: none en route
How to get there: 🚗 Turn off the Isola San Biagio/Montefortino road (south of Amandola, the 81km-point on Car tour 8) for Rubbiano. Past the village follow the wide track west into the Tenna Valley for

To the west of Amandola the Tenna torrent has etched a steep gorge, the Gola dell'Infernaccio, into the limestone of the Monti Sibillini. This outing leads along easily-walkable trails and paths between the steep cliffs of 'Hell's Gorge'. On the return we come to a lovely resting spot by the recently-built chapel of San Leonardo. A single hermit monk living up here in total seclusion completed it all by himself after years of hard work.

From the **parking place** follow the main track straight on, down to the Tenna, and cross on a **wooden foot-bridge** (**10 min**). Then take a trail which passes the entrance to a tunnel on the right. You rise alongside the stream (red and white waymarks of CAI Route 10). Just at the start of the gorge the torrent rushes down through a rocky cleft. The trail then follows the watercourse through shady beech woods. Ignore Route 11 turning right uphill towards San Leonardo (**45min**); keep to the pleasant trail gently climbing the valley floor for a good 30 minutes. The steep cliffs of Monte Priora (2332m) and Monte Sibilla (2173m)

San Leonardo

tower above you. Eventually the dark side-ravine of **Fosso le Vene** opens up to the south (**1h30min**), often snow-filled until May.
Turn back here and retrace your steps for just under 1km. Having crossed the torrent four times, take a path forking off left *(no waymarks)*. This rises northeast along the wooded slopes. After around 15 minutes the path, somewhat over-grown in places, meets a wider path coming up from the gorge on the right (CAI Route 11, passed earlier). Climbing up left here; after a good five minutes you reach the hermit's chapel, **San Leonardo** (**2h05min**). A single hermit still lives up here, tending some little gardens at the edge of the gorge. A meadow by a drinking water spring makes a good place for a break.
Leave this peaceful place by retracing your steps for around five minutes, then go left, keeping on Route 11. This zigzags downhill through beeches, back to Route 10 in the bottom of the valley. Retrace your steps, back to the **parking place** (**3h**).

Walk 33: IN THE MONTI DELLA LAGA NEAR ACQUASANTA

Photograph on page 44
Distance/time: 18km; 5h15min
Grade: moderate, with an overall ascent/descent of 650m, no severe ascents; easy orientation

Equipment: as pages 46-47
Refreshments: none en route
How to get there: 🚌 to Umito (shortly before the 194km point on Car tour 8); no public transport

Thick deciduous woods of chestnut and beech cover the steep northern slopes of the Monti della Laga. Large areas of this remote region are wilderness, with no tracks or trails, where the Italian Partisans had their hideouts during the Second World War. The only paths are beside the streams flowing down from the high mountains. This walk follows the course of the Fosso della Montagna; focal points are two picturesque waterfalls with basins, whirlpools, and rock faces smoothed by running water.

Start out in **Umito** (690m), where the road up from Acquasanta ends at a turning area below a church. Some 20m beyond a little building with a fountain, take a track turning right downhill towards the valley of the Fosso della Montagna (☞: Volpara). Keep to the main route, with the stream on your right. At a footbridge the track narrows a little and soon climbs more steeply. After some ups and downs you come to a clear right-hand bend, where you cross a **side stream** (764m; **50min**). Now divert left on a steep narrow path, following a stream into a side-valley. Past some smooth bedrock and a wooded section strewn with large erratic boulders, you come to the 50m-high, stepped **Cascata della Prata** (890m; **1h15min**).

Retrace your steps to the main trail (**1h30min**). In 10 minutes you pass a little building on the left and the trail narrows to a path. Sheltered by beeches and chestnuts you steadily gain height. You pass a little **cave** with an old oven (**2h**). Twenty minutes later you cross a side-stream, which joins as a pretty little waterfall. The path then rises more steeply and passes smooth rock faces. The **Cascata della Volpara** soon comes into view on the right (1180m; **3h10min**). Only in spring, when the snows melt, does a real waterfall pour down. At other times

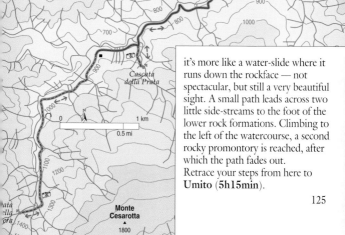

it's more like a water-slide where it runs down the rockface — not spectacular, but still a very beautiful sight. A small path leads across two little side-streams to the foot of the lower rock formations. Climbing to the left of the watercourse, a second rocky promontory is reached, after which the path fades out.
Retrace your steps from here to **Umito** (**5h15min**).

125

Walk 34: COLLE SAN MARCO, NEAR ASCOLI PICENO

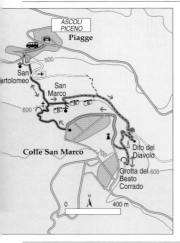

Distance/time: 6.5km; 2h
Grade: easy; ascent/descent 250m
Equipment: see pages 46-47; sturdy shoes are sufficient
Refreshments: bar near the 1h20min-point
How to get there: 🚌 to Piagge, south of Ascoli Piceno (end of Car tour 8). In Piagge drive to the uppermost part of the village, to a parking area on the left side of the road (150m beyond a sharp left-hand bend and before the turn-off to the hotel Villa Scariglia). 🚌 from Ascoli Piceno to Colle San Marco Mon-Sat 6 times daily (ex Sundays); Info: www. startspa.it
Note: On weekends there are many day-trippers in the area.

The mountain range of Montagna dei Fiori, rising to the south of the picturesque town of Ascoli Piceno, has been a refuge of mystics and hermits since early medieval times. The deserted Eremo San Marco, the goal of this short walk, clings dramatically to the steep rock-face. Below the monastery the thick deciduous forest has a fine stands of ancient sweet chestnut trees.

Start the walk in **Piagge**: turn onto the side road ascending past the hotel Villa Scariglia. At the next junction go left and walk up the steps to the 14th-century **Chiesa di San Bartolomeo**. Behind the church continue straight on along a wood-

land trail rising to the **cemetery**. Walking to the right of the cemetery enclosure, you come to a junction, where you take the trail climbing straight ahead *(not waymarked)*. This cobbled mule trail steadily gains height. At the following Y-fork

Ascoli Piceno: the Piazza dei Popolo

View from the Eremo San Marco down to Ascoli Piceno

(**20min**), go left (⌐: Eremo San Marco).

The pleasant woodland trail leads within five minutes to concrete steps. These ascend across a deep crevice to the **hermitage of San Marco** built against a vertical rock face. The monastery's gate is normally open, and you can climb all the way up to a cave with an altar. From here you look through Romanesque windows down to Ascoli Piceno at the foot of Monte Ascensione.

Going from the lower end of the staircase 50m to the right, you step onto a rocky promontory (**40min**), offering a good view to the rock face with the monastery *(take care; steep drops!)*. The ongoing route, however, descends the path opposite the steps. This zigzags down through dark woods. 'Attenzione' — signposts forbid the gathering of chestnuts. At any unclear junctions, keep to the right (⌐: Dito del Diavolo). In the shade of sweet chestnut trees you come to a **clearing** with a view to the rock face of San Marco. The path forking off right here, despite being signposted (⌐: Torretta-Corrado) *ends* after 50m at a wall in the woods; instead, follow the main path 50m to the left, to a T-junction (**50min**).

Turn right (⌐: Grotta B. Corrado), to follow a path leading uphill through woods (now mainly beech). Veering right, you eventually emerge on a meadow with a single chestnut tree, surrounded by a ring of stones (**1h**). Walk to the right of the tree and continue 150m, to a tumbledown shed. From here take a path off to the right. Beyond a sharp left-hand bend, this leads to the right of the isolated rock tower known as **Dito del Diavolo** (Devil's Finger). In the dark patch of woods behind the rock, go 50m to the left, to a flat area where a steeply-stepped path begins on the right.

Make a **diversion** here: first follow the path continuing straight on. After 100m, by a ruined wall on the left (the scant remains of a medieval monastery), the path veers right and rises to a small opening in the steep rock face, the entrance to a tiny hermit's cave, the **Grotta del Beato Corrado** (**1h10min**).

Back at the flat area, take the stepped path to the left, climbing the steep wooded slopes. At **Colle San Marco** you meet a tarred road (**1h20min**), where you turn right. *(But perhaps first call at the bar 250m to the left.)* Follow the road for about 10 minutes, past a **monument to the Partisans** (Sacrario Partigiani) and two side- roads forking off to the left, to come to house No 11. Take the downhill track opposite the house; this passes two round concrete buildings on the left and narrows to a path. You descend through a forest of mixed oaks for 10 minutes, to some rocks in the woods, where a deep cave opens up on the left. The route, now an old cobbled pilgrims' trail, veers right, passes a niche in a rock with a little Madonna, and comes back to the fork first encountered at the 20min-point (**1h45min**). Retrace your steps back to **Piagge** (**2h**).

127

Walk 35: ON MONTAGNA DEI FIORI NEAR ASCOLI PICENO

Distance/time: 9km; 3h
Grade: easy, with an overall ascent/descent of 480m; easy orientation; a short stony stretch after 20min needs a little care in wet conditions
Equipment: as pages 46-47
Refreshments: only in San Giacomo; none en route
How to get there: 🚌 south from

Ascoli Piceno (where Car tour 8 ends); in San Giacomo take the earthen road to Tre Maciare (to the left of the surfaced road down to San Vito). This ends after 3km ends at a little ski lift. No public transport
Walking map: I Monti Gemelli, Carta dei Sentieri 1:25,000, Club Alpino Ascoli Piceno; available at the hotels in San Giacomo

The Montagna dei Fiori, the 'mountains of flowers', were named for the many crocuses which flower on these grassy slopes in spring. In the south the range rises steadily up to the flat panoramic 1814m-high summit of Monte Girella. From these treeless heights you can see for hundreds of kilometres on a clear day — all the way to the highest ranges of the Apennine peninsula and a long stretch of the Adriatic coastline. A special feature of these mountains are the primitive drystone stone huts, built from stones collected in the fields. For centuries these *caciare* were used as simple sleeping places for the itinerant herdsmen.

Start out from the little **lift station**: walk back 300m along the unsurfaced road, then take a trail to the left. Descend a short way, past a building with a tiled roof, then gain height along the western hillside. You pass a first *caciare,* 50m below on the right. To the west you have a long view over the mountain ranges of the Monti Sibillini and Monti della Laga, both rising to around 2500m. The trail narrows to a path (**20min**) and descends for three minutes across stony terrain at the foot of a steep limestone cliff. Climbing again, you walk through a small beech wood. At the end of the wood you emerge on the meadows of the high valley of **Vallone** rising to the southeast (**35min**). Following a pleasant path running along the grassy slopes 50m to the left above the valley bed, you gain height steadily. Another *caciare* comes up on the right. Veering right, you pass a third *caciare,* again on the right, and come onto a small **high plain** with a fourth *caciare* near a **round pond**. This pond doesn't dry up even in high summer, which

allows some tiny sweetwater crayfish to live in the water (1625m; **1h15min**). To the south and west you enjoy a large panoramic view to Abruzzi, from near Montagna dei Campi (1718m) to far-off Corno Grande (2912m), the highest mountain in all the Apennines. Continue straight on for five more minutes on the path along the western hillside (🚩: Sorgente Girella) and then veer right, to the edge of the mountain: now you can see how the rounded hilltops of the Montagna dei Fiori drop down with steep cliffs towards the Castellano Valley.
Return to the pond, then take the path which climbs the grassy slopes diagonally to the east (🚩: Montagna dei Fiori). You rise onto a flat saddle (1764m; **1h50min**). Head right here, over treeless terrain; within 10 minutes you're on the flat summit of **Monte Girella** (1814m; **2h**), another superb panoramic viewpoint, from where a stretch of coastline also comes into view.
Retrace your steps to the saddle, then take a faint trail straight ahead

Above: view from the Montagna dei Fiori to the west; left: a drystone caciare

across the open ridge (■: 402 Tre Caciare). After having climbed gently for five minutes, you descend steeply into a hollow (1706m), where a more distinct trail begins. Follow this a short way uphill, to a ski-lift, and walk along beside it to a transmitting mast (**2h40min**).

Past the mast, descend straight ahead across a steeply-sloping meadow. Cross a track, veer a little to the right, and continue to the edge of the woods, where you can pick up a woodland trail that begins by a little yellow signpost. Follow this downhill in the shade of beeches. After a left-hand bend you pass **Tre Maciare**, a hillock on the right with three more *caciare*. From here it's only 150m back to the starting point at the **lift station** (**3h**).

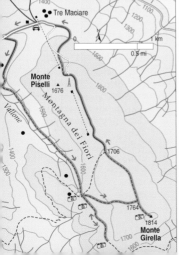

129

Walk 36: THROUGH THE GOLA DI SALINELLO

Distance/time: 6km; 2h
Grade: easy, but with several stream crossings on stepping stones
Equipment: as pages 46-47
Refreshments: none en route
How to get there: 🚗 to Ripe (south of Ascoli Piceno, where Car tour 8 ends). Where the road bends above the church at Ripe, take the dirt road signposted to Grotta S. Angelo, which ends 1.5km further on at a

From Monte Girella the mountains of the Montagna dei Fiori drop steeply to the south. Below, the Salinello torrent winds its way through a wooded gorge formed by vertical rock walls. We walk through this remote gorge on a fairly easy path. At the start of the walk, the little cave-church of Sant'Angelo is another reminder of medieval hermit life in the Montagna dei Fiori.

Start out at the **parking area**: take the descending main track (⁅: Grotta S. Angelo, Route 412). This narrows and runs above the Salinello Valley, protected by a wooden railing. After a short walk to the right, two openings appear in the cliffs 50m above, with small paths leading up to them. The right-hand path climbs an iron staircase to the spacious hermits' cave, **Grotta Sant'Angelo** (**15min**), where an altar testifies to its use as place of Christian worship.

At the end of the Salinello Gorge

Return to the main path; after three minutes, turn left at a signposted junction (⁅: Vroga delle Trocche 587m). The path descends some wooden stairs for five minutes, to another junction in front of a low macchia-covered hill, where a **diversion** to the left down a steep narrow path leads to the **Salinello stream** — by a little waterfall pouring down a 20m high rock face into a stone basin (10 minutes there and back). The main path, to the right, reaches the point 30m ahead where the Salinello forces its way through some rocks above the waterfall (**35min**).

Following red/yellow/red way-marked Route 412 straight on, you walk deeper into the valley. A little later the high cliffs of the **Gola di Salinello** tower above the path. You walk through a dark wood, on the left bank of the stream. You cross the stream twice in quick succession (by some stone basins). Ignore the path forking right towards Santa Maria Scalena (**50min**); instead, climb a short way left up some stone steps. Then continue upstream for around 15 more minutes, crossing the stream several times on stepping stones. Eventually the vertical rock faces close up, and suddenly the **end of the gorge** is reached (**1h10min**).

Retracing your steps, walk back to the **parking area** (**2h**).

Walk 37: ABOVE THE SEA ON MONTE CONERO

Distance/time: 11km; 3h45min
Grade: easy-moderate, with an overall ascent of 380m; quite easy orientation (several signposts)
Equipment: as pages 46-47; sturdy shoes on account of the stony terrain; swimming things
Refreshments: bar/restaurant at Badia San Pietro; bar/trattoria on San Michele Beach (summer only)
How to get there: 🚌 From Piazza Stamira in the centre of Ancona take town bus 93 (Massignano bus) as far as the Osteria del Poggio at Poggio di Ancona (8 buses on working days, only 3 on Sundays; info: www. conerobus.it). Return on 🚌 from Sirolo to Ancona (Reni bus company; on working days about 15, on Sundays only about 5 buses; info: www.anconarenibus.it); the bus stop in Sirolo is on the main road below the centre, near the main church (bus shelter); tickets are available at the *tabacchi* near the main square.
Variation 1 — Sirolo circuit: 10km; 3h45min; moderate. 🚌 to/

from Sirolo (info: www. anconarenibus.it). **Start out** at the **cemetery in Sirolo**, at the northern edge of the town. (This is reached from the town centre in 15 minutes by taking Via Cave/Via Vallone past hotel Beatrice.) Take the small road climbing from the cemetery to the left through olive groves. Passing the entrance to Villa Carlo, you come to the Monte Conero road, which you walk straight down for 100m, to the Sirolo/Ancona road. Walk 50m to the right, then, past the bar-trattoria, take a side-road off right. After 150m you pass an old kiln with a tiled chimney. Walking Route 5 to Pian di Raggetti starts behind this, just to the right of the gate to house No 22. Initially it runs as an cleared path through thorny undergrowth and eventually veers right to a track (**20min**). Turning left, you pass three old quarries. At the third quarry the route curves sharp left and starts climbing more steeply. Then, after veering right (north), it

leads less steeply through a patch of woods onto the grassy plain of **Pian di Raggetti**. At its uppermost end, you come to the crossroads at the 1h-point in the main walk (**1h20min**).

Just before continuing to the right on Route 1, back to Sirolo, turn left for a **diversion** north on Route 1, to the **superb viewpoint** above the steep coast of Portonovo (the 40min-point in the main walk; 40 minutes there and back from Pian di Raggetti). Then follow the main walk from the 1h-point to the end.

Variation 2 — from Sirolo to Due Sorelle: 8km; 2h45min; difficult: you must be sure-footed and have a head for heights (the skiddy path from Passo del Lupo down to the sea is very steep and exposed). Access as Variation 1.

From the **cemetery at Sirolo** follow the track ascending to the left of the enclosure walls. Rising past the entrance to a villa, you come to a major crossroads, where you turn

right (ℸ: Due Sorelle Sentiero 1/2). After 100m Route 1 turns off left (**25min**); keep straight ahead here on Route 2 (the main track). At a villa on the right around five minutes later, climb a short way to the left, to some gnarled old olive trees. Then continue on a lovely flat path, with occasional glimpses over the coast at Sirolo. A good ten minutes from the villa you leave the woods and emerge on the open panoramic ridge of **Passo del Lupo** (**45min**), with views down over the steep coast. From here waymarked Route 2 drops steeply towards the sea. Although ropes help on the trickiest sections, this path is tough; *take care not to cause rockfalls*. At the bottom you step onto the lovely beach of **Due Sorelle**, edged by two limestone stacks rising from the sea (**1h20min**). Retrace your steps up to **Sirolo** (**2h45min**).

Walking map: Carta Escursionistica Parco del Conero, 1:20,000

The flat Adriatic coast of the Marche, with its dead straight shorelines full of holiday places, campsites and hotels is definitely *not* an area for lovely walks through unspoilt nature. Only the small coastal mountain range of Monte Conero, a nature reserve on the doorstep of Ancona, breaks the scenic monotony. This walk follows small tracks, trails and paths through typical Mediterranean macchia with evergreen shrubby woods, the sweet-scented pines and broom-filled meadows shining bright yellow in early summer. At several points we enjoy superb views down to the sea and the steeply-dropping coastal slopes. There's a chance to swim, too, at Sirolo's San Michele beach.

Starting point is in the upper part of the village of **Poggio di Ancona**, by the restaurant Osteria del Poggio (bus stop). Take the lane climbing to the right (south) of the restaurant. Some 50m further on, at the houses 53 and 54, this becomes a hiking path and leads uphill in the shade of pines and holm oaks. At a fork five minutes up, turn left. Ten more minutes of ascent along a pleasant path takes you to a track (**15min**). This keeps rising east along the slopes of Monte Conero through

dark green macchia. When the track flattens out, a wooden guard-rail and an explanation board come into view on the left. Climb a few paces up the bank here. From the edge of the slope, you suddenly look down on the **steep coast** above Portonovo Bay, where the Romanesque church of Santa Maria stands by the shore. Follow the railing another 250m to the right, past more superb viewpoints.

At the junction at the end of the railing (**40min**), turn right (⚐: Pian di Raggetti Sentiero 1). You now contour the wooded hillside, veering left. The forest finally thins out and you come to the upper edge of the **Pian di Raggetti** (**1h**), a sloping grassy plateau full of broom and pines, offering a long view to the shoreline of Sirolo and over undulating hills — an ideal spot for a picnic.

At the **crossroads** here continue straight ahead on Route 1 (⚐: Ex Convento Camaldolesi), which soon passes a ruin on the left. The trail climbs a little and traverses the southern slopes of Monte Conero, partly through holm oak woods and partly with views over the surroundings. Skirting a fence, you join a tarmac track. Follow this straight on for three minutes, to the side-road coming up from Sirolo.

Due Sorelle Beach

Follow this road uphill for five minutes, to the **Badia San Pietro** (**1h30min**). Today this small medieval monastery is a three-star hotel. The monastery church is built in Romanesque style, with fine sculptures on the capitals.

Your ongoing route, Route 1 to Sirolo, begins just to the left of the monastery walls. The shady, easily-walked path leaves the holm oak woods around 10 minutes from Badia San Pietro. From a viewpoint with a handrail called '**Belvedere**', you have a fine view down to the sea. Continue on a path beyond a concrete post, descending to the left through shrubs. Ignore the following turn-off to the right. The path, stony in places, zigzags south downhill past two more viewpoints. A little later it veers a little to the right, in a more westerly direction. After a left-hand bend, you come to the left turning of a small path numbered 1c. Take this: it brings you within three minutes to a low rock face in the woods, at the end of which is the narrow entrance to a hermits' cave called **Grotta Mortarolo** (**2h15min**).

Retrace your steps back to the main

route (Route 1), which continues west downhill through Mediterranean vegetation, then widens out and joins a track behind a villa. Follow the track straight ahead, gently uphill, to a **major crossroads** (**2h30min**). Turn left here, now keeping to Route 2 and a track going downhill to the **cemetery at Sirolo** (**2h45min**).

Continuing straight ahead on the road, you would reach the centre of Sirolo within 15 minutes. But it's more interesting to make a short diversion via San Michele Beach: turn left on a side road 100m beyond the cemetery (⌐: Sentiero dei Sassi Neri). After 250m, with a view down to the sea, turn left on a track. At the two following junctions go right, to descend towards the coast in the shade of pines. After a another curve, branch off right, to follow a smaller track down the wooded hillside. At the right-hand bend 20m before the end of the small wood (where the sea comes into view and there is a small fire hydrant on the right), fork left on a path. This heads down more steeply, then veers left through a stand of maritime pines and into a gully. A little tricky walking of 50m down the gully is needed before you can step onto the beach, **Spiaggia San Michele** (**3h15min**).

You now tramp across the pebbles of the beach for just under 500m, until you reach Route 4, a path with a wooden railing climbing steeply up to the right. (It's easy to miss this path; if you come to the path up to Camping Internazionale you have gone too far!) Route 4 zigzags uphill as a forest trail and takes you to the public park, **Giardino Pubblico**, and then the main square next to the church in **Sirolo** (**3h45min**).

Index

Geographical names comprise the only entries in this Index. For other entries, see Contents, page 3. A page number in *italic type* indicates a map reference; a page number in **bold type** indicates a photograph. Both of these may be in addition to a text reference on the same page.

135